Don't Die Before Paris

by

Alexis Powers

Dedicated to:

My family and my daughters, Elizabeth and Madeleine. Each one has helped me through many difficult situations, never letting me down, even when my behavior was beyond the normal realm. I am grateful to them and to the scores of loyal friends who have stood by me and loved me, no matter what.

I hope this memoir explains some of my bizarre behavior through the years.

A special thanks to Caryn Lennon and Rayford Hammond for their editorial services, and to Kevin Engellenner for book cover design.

Memories

Like the tide, they roll in,
Then roll out,
They appear as Waves Crashing
Sometimes rough, Sometimes calm

Memories
Feel so real, so painful
As if they were happening again
And again

Memories of a wonderful father,
His laugh, his honesty, his sense of fun.

And the other men, lots of other men,
Sexy ones, successful ones, funny ones
And not so funny ones.

Memories of Mom
A yearning to feel loved
A yearning to be accepted
Yearnings finally realized.

Memories of two little girls,
Innocent, beautiful, humorous and smart
Women now
Are they happy? Do they smile?
Have they forgiven the cause of their terrible childhood?

Memories of Shep, Terri,
Lucy, Buster and now
Toots and Charlie
Love freely given

When do memories end?
Do they cease rolling in and rolling out?
When is the mind quiet, calm and serene?
When do I sleep?

Don't Die Before Paris
A Mother's Memoir

It's one of those amazing miracles of life that my daughters still speak to me. They tell me they've forgiven me. They obviously have more forgiving personalities than I do.

Ah, guilt. I've got massive quantities of it. It's the only possible way to feel after what I put my kids through. They have lots of reasons to be resentful. Some women are born mothers. Some women are terrific caretakers. I don't fall into either one of those categories. I should have been a movie star so my children could have been raised by loving, responsible nannies. Instead of a self-sacrificing loving parent, they had a mother too immature to understand the complexities and responsibilities of motherhood. Instead of the Mother of the Year, they had the *mother from hell.*

In my defense, you have to know that I didn't start out bad. First of all, I was a breech case. My mother often said, "She came out backwards, and proceeded to do everything backwards. If I told her to wear the blue dress, she wore the red dress.

Nothing ever changed." It wasn't until I started writing this memoir that I learned from my 91-year-old mother how she outsmarted me. It turns out that if she wanted me to wear the blue dress, she told me to wear the red dress, using my contrary nature to get me to do what she thought best. I learned the art of manipulation at the hands of a master, though I didn't realize it at the time. Anyway, I sure learned how to become a conniving adult.

Aside from that, when I was young, I was the homely girl who didn't have friends, the sickly kid that grownups felt sorry for, the girl with one eyebrow straight across (think of Frida Khalo), freckles, green tinted hair (my only sport was swimming, too much chlorine in the water) and buck teeth caused by falling down the stairs when I was about two, something my mother never forgave me for doing. I was the smart, ugly one, the one the other kids despised. Nobody expected much from me; it was my brother who was supposed to accomplish great things. Which he did. In a big way.

To escape my sad, lonely life, I grew up with my nose in a book, which turned out to be a very good thing, but I'll get to that later. The library was a safe haven. School was easy for me, mainly because I could remember everything I heard or read. Besides swimming, all I wanted to do was read, so it was easy to get good grades. I breezed through, graduating from high school at 16. High school was not pleasant. When you're two years younger than the other girls, you're getting better grades and you don't wear a bra, kids make fun of you. They can be really mean.

Then the miracle occurred. The ugly duckling phase finally ended. The braces came off; I lost ten pounds and I could fill a B cup. When I looked in the mirror, a beautiful raven-haired swan with hazel eyes stared back at me. Could this gorgeous creature really be me? I fell in love. With myself.

Elizabeth Taylor was a bit taller, but otherwise we could have been twins. People quite often remarked about the resemblance. I didn't see it, but I didn't argue. Black hair, beautiful eyes, creamy skin and a body to die for. Anytime there was a camera in sight, I would willingly put on fresh lipstick, pose and deliver that million dollar smile. (After having most of my teeth capped, it was close to a million dollar smile.) Women either hated me or envied me; for years men would fall all over themselves to have me. Not that I cared. The more they wanted me, the worse I treated them. Jack Suarez did manage to capture me, however, and he became the father of my two girls, Lizzie and Madi, formally known as Elizabeth and Madeleine.

So here's what happened from the time their father died until they graduated from high school. As a famous actress in an Academy Award winning performance once said, "Fasten your seatbelts, it will be a bumpy ride."

Chapter 1
Leaving Los Angeles

My mother, as I mentioned, is 91. Until very recently she lived alone, went to the casino once a week, played Canasta and refused to give up driving until she wound up in the hospital and finally admitted she needed help. As of this writing, she has a live-in caretaker. Now the two of them go to the casino but Mom has finally given up driving. Even now she is fond of saying things like, "Everything happens for the best," or "God has a plan for you," or "There's a reason for everything." That is not always true. Things do not always happen for the best. The adage that "God helps those who help themselves" makes a lot more sense to me.

The first week I spent with Jack Suarez in Los Angeles, he was sick. If God was in charge, he was giving me a clue. But did I pay any attention to this enormous head's up? No. I thought I was in love. Instead of telling him I had to return to San Francisco, I stayed in Los Angeles and took care of him. When he told me he'd had heart surgery years ago, did I think ahead to what this might mean?

No. I offered him a cup of hot tea. After two weeks he recovered. But it was temporary.

There are many things that happen that make no sense and have no reasonable explanation. Looking back, it is obvious my choices could have been more sensible. After a few months of flying back and forth from San Francisco to Los Angeles (one day I flew back and forth twice because I forgot something I needed), Jack convinced me to leave San Francisco and move to Los Angeles. He proposed. I accepted.

During the time we were married, he was constantly suffering from his heart disease. I've come to believe we create our own environment. Hard to explain why I married a man who had a serious chronic illness. On the other hand, if I had not married Jack, I would not have two beautiful, wonderful daughters. So, what does it all mean? I still don't have the answer.

Jack died in 1977 at the age of 46. At the time of his death he and I were divorced, he had remarried and our daughters were in his custody. There's no need to get into the gory details of what caused our divorce and why Jack had custody of our daughters. When Jack insisted he wanted custody, I agreed, not aware of the devastating effect it would have on my daughters, not to mention me.

When Jack succumbed to heart disease, Liz was 13 and Madi was 12. On the day he passed away, his wife, Marilyn, had left him alone to fill a needed prescription. Although he was rarely home by himself, Madi was the one who found him dead on the kitchen floor. It was one of a series of very bad days for my poor daughters.

Even though everyone knew Jack's time was limited, no one talked about what would happen to the children when he died. For a long time I had wanted custody. Whenever I asked Jack to let me have the girls, he adamantly refused. I assumed they would come to live with me after Jack's demise. Never assume anything. Get it in writing. After his death I learned that Marilyn intended to keep the girls, ignoring the fact that I was their mother.

During the years Marilyn and Jack were together, the children stayed with me every other weekend and I had them for two weeks during the summer. We alternated holidays. To broaden their horizons I took them to museums, concerts, expensive restaurants and bought them beautiful clothes. To this day they thank me for introducing them to classical music, art and teaching them which fork to use. After my lessons they could attend a formal White House dinner and never be confused by the cutlery!

Even though Marilyn and I knew each other before Jack started fooling around with her, our relationship deteriorated as time went on. She and I avoided each other as much as possible.

Jack's illness had taken a toll not only on his wife but also on Liz and Madi, especially for the past three years. When he was unable to go to work and needed a lot of attention, they helped Marilyn take care of him. They were considerate of his illness when he was home, not making too much noise, not inviting friends over. A lot of the attention and care they should have received was diverted. This information was passed on to me by the girls when we were together. Now that I look back I should have gone to court to get custody. I should have done a lot of things.

The morning after Jack died Marilyn called to tell me he'd passed away. I was shocked even though I knew death was imminent. The last time I'd picked the children up he'd answered the door. Although at one time he'd been handsome, that day he could have passed for 70 years old. When Marilyn asked me not to attend his funeral, I agreed.

There was a man in my life I had dated off and on for several years who loved Liz and Madi. Confused, I wasn't sure how to handle the situation with Marilyn and so I called him for advice. Bluntly, without much conversation, he told me, "Whatever it takes, get your daughters."

The girls and I had planned a trip to Connecticut that summer because my sister, Lisa, was getting married to Jon Belle. My brother, Mel, was hosting the wedding in his huge backyard in New Fairfield, Connecticut. He lived a block and a half away from my folks. Airline tickets had been purchased for our vacation; all the arrangements were in place. As it turned out, it was a blessing that Jack died about ten days before we were scheduled to leave.

Marilyn agreed that I could pick the girls up from the Friday night service at the synagogue. During our marriage Jack told me he thought his grandmother was Jewish. To this day I don't know if he was telling the truth. The few times I articulated that I found his being Jewish strange since his name was Suarez, he explained they were Sephardic Jews. Once he told me they were forced to lie about being Jewish because of the Crusades. I never could believe a word Jack said about anything. Lying was a way of life for him. Based on his proclamation that he was Jewish, we joined a synagogue and he eventually became president of the Men's Club.

Marilyn was taking the girls to Sabbath services that Friday night because they would mention

Jack's name. For moral support, I asked my friend Charlotte to accompany me to the service. We acted as if we were picking the girls up for the two week vacation. After the service, the girls said goodbye to Marilyn, retrieved their suitcases from her car and we left. The girls and Marilyn did not know they would not see each other again.

Charlotte and I drove to my apartment on Lafayette Park Place. Liz and Madi slept in my queen bed, Charlotte slept on the couch and I put two easy chairs together. Sometimes there are benefits to being short. All the girls had with them were enough clothes for two weeks. The next morning Charlotte drove us to the airport. My parents and my brother picked us up in New York. My mom was overjoyed to see us. My brother drove us to my parents' home in New Fairfield, Connecticut.

That night, when the children were asleep, I talked to my parents, explaining the situation with Marilyn. "Why not stay here with us?" my mom asked. "We have three bedrooms, you can use one and the girls can share one. You won't have to pay rent. You'll get on your feet. The children can go to school and you'll find a job."

"If I didn't think Marilyn would give us problems, I'd never consider moving here but I don't trust her," I said truthfully.

"Look," my mom said, a serious tone to her voice, "your apartment is too small for the three of you so you don't even have a place to live. School starts soon. Why don't we give it a try?"

For some bizarre reason, this sounded like the perfect solution to a big problem. But how could I just dismiss the great job I had at a Los Angeles law firm? How could I think that moving the children from California to Connecticut so soon after losing their home and father would be a good thing? Why would a rational adult make such an idiotic decision? Oddly enough, there were occasions when my brain simply ceased to function. And, of course, there was something else behind my poor judgment. Alcohol.

After we were living with my folks for a couple of weeks, the girls began asking when we were going home. They said they missed their friends. In retrospect, I can see how frightened they must have been. They were teenagers, going through raging hormonal changes, away from their friends and familiar surroundings. Everything they'd known for over ten years had been taken away. Living in the home of my parents, although they were generous, kind and loving, was difficult for all of us. Meanwhile, friends in California were cleaning out my apartment, putting my furniture in storage, and taking care of the odds and ends I'd left behind. Coward that I was, instead of informing Liz and Madi that the move to Connecticut might be permanent, I decided to wait to break the news to them hoping that at some point I would figure out how to tell them without it being traumatic. Another one of my brilliant decisions!

Marilyn started calling my parents' home. At first, I let her speak to the girls. But the fourth time she called, the children were asleep. I told her we were staying in Connecticut. When she started screaming at me that they were *her* daughters, I advised her that she had no legal claim to *my* daughters. Although she didn't mention getting an attorney, by this time I'd started to worry that she would hire a lawyer and we'd have to endure a lengthy custody battle. I knew there was less chance of a custody fight if we were on the other side of the country. That was one of the major reasons for us to stay in Connecticut.

Eventually Liz and Madi noticed there was no talk of returning to California. "Aren't we doing back to Marilyn," Lizzie asked, Madi standing close to her sister, listening.

Feebly I tried explaining to the girls, "We're staying here. I'm registering you for school."

First, they looked at each other. They're only eleven months apart and sometimes seem like twins. Then they began to cry.

"Listen," I said, my stomach feeling like the world was caving in, "give it a chance. We're in a bad position."

"What about our furniture and all our stuff?" Lizzie said. "And we hardly have any clothes with us."

"We'll buy you new clothes," I said, wondering to myself how we would manage. I had no income.

Without saying anything they ran toward their room, leaving me standing in the kitchen. Frustrated, unhappy, annoyed with life, I sighed. What I really wanted was a great big scotch and soda, heavy on the scotch, light on the soda, but even *I* didn't start drinking until four in the afternoon. Unless of course it was the weekend.

Slowly, my heart heavy with doubt and despair, I followed them to their room, gently knocking on the closed door. For a few moments I heard nothing. Then there was some movement. Madi opened the door, her eyes red from crying. Her soft blond hair stuck to her face, her blue eyes were bloodshot, and there was a look of complete despair on her angelic face. They let me into their room.

I sat down on the bed, cradling them in my lap, the way I had when they were two and three years old. I cried as I explained how much I had missed them for the years they lived with Jack.

"I've wanted you to live with me for a long time. Now that your dad is gone, you will stay with me. We'll have fun together."

"What about Marilyn?" Madi asked.

"Do you want to go back to living with Marilyn instead of living with me?"

As if they'd received an electric shock, they sat up, staring at each other. Finally I got what was going on in their minds. They didn't realize they had a choice.

"What is it?" I asked.

And then they told me the truth. For the years they'd lived with Jack and Marilyn, Jack has been an overbearing, unreasonable and cruel parent. And Marilyn had participated. There were beatings, there was screaming and many times they were sent to their room without dinner. Marilyn and Jack would not let them wear the beautiful clothes I purchased for them. They couldn't make any noise in the house. They'd had a terrible life.

I started to cry and pulled them toward me.

"Why didn't you tell me?" I asked.

"We were afraid to," Madi sobbed.

For a few moments all three of us said nothing, immersed in our thoughts. I felt my heart break into a million pieces. I hated myself, thinking of all the nights of going out dancing, drinking and having a good time while my own daughters were being tortured. Feelings of guilt smothered me, something I would not be free of for the rest of my life.

After a few moments, they put their arms around me, telling me that they loved me and were glad they'd never see Marilyn again. Liz got a tissue and wiped the tears from my face. Then these two adorable girls told me not to worry. (Why were two young teenagers telling their mother not to worry?) Their lives had been shattered but I could tell they wanted me to be happy. Their blue eyes sparkled as they spoke.

"Okay, mom, we'll give it a chance," Liz said. Madi chimed in with, "We'll start school here in New Fairfield. Don't worry, Mom, we won't even ask you for money for anything. Maybe we can get jobs." (Jobs? They were only 12 and 13!)

I felt they were too young to understand that one of the reasons we were staying in Connecticut was that I could not emotionally or financially handle a custody battle with Marilyn, even though I was pretty sure I would prevail. After hearing what their life was like with Marilyn and Jack, I thought any mention of a custody battle would terrify them. As it did me.

Before I could say anything else, Lizzie said, "Can we get our ears pierced?" Even at a young age, Liz knew how to take advantage of a situation.

For the last two or three years they would complain that Jack would not allow them to pierce their ears. All of their friends had pierced ears when they were about ten years old. When they'd beg me to let them pierce their ears, I told them Jack had to give permission. Now he was no longer around. With a big smile on my face, I said, "Yes, we will get your ears pierced this week." Both of them smiled as they became immediately aware that their lives would get better. The very next day my mom and I drove them into the small town, found a place where ears were pierced and bought them each three pairs of earrings. They were ecstatic.

Each morning, I vigilantly read the want ads. This was before computers, cell phones and all the hi-tech stuff we now take for granted. Jobs were scarce in the Danbury area. Back in California, I had a job with Hughes Hubbard & Reed, a prestigious New York law firm with a branch office in downtown Los Angeles. My boss was liaison counsel for Atlantic Richfield in the oil industry anti-trust case. Even though I planned to stay in Connecticut, I had avoided telling the law firm I would not return.

As time passed, I realized that my subconscious must have known I wasn't totally committed to remain in Connecticut or I would have severed ties with the law firm. And I would have made arrangements to have my car shipped back East. The more I searched for a job in the area, the more I realized there was no way I could replace the high powered job I had or earn the salary paid by Hughes Hubbard, unless I was willing to travel back and forth to New York City by train each day. But I kept on looking, listening to my mother's words that everything happens for a reason. Pshaw!

Chapter 2

The Sausage Incident

The days dragged on and on and on. When Madi came home from school she cried, saying she was being bullied and made fun of. My boss in Los Angeles called constantly, asking when I was coming back to work. I was not ready to break the news to him. That job was my backup. Friends in Los Angeles called asking me when I planned to return. The good news was that Marilyn had stopped calling. Mutual friends advised me that their house had been sold and Marilyn had moved out of the area. Other than that information, the world looked bleak.

My best friend was four o'clock, the start of the cocktail hour. Every time I poured myself a drink, my mother scrutinized me, her eyebrows went up and although she didn't say anything I could feel her disapproval from the top of my head to the bottom of my feet. My parents never drank. The only time I saw my father a bit tipsy was at the Passover Seder.

Moving back home with your parents after you've been away for twenty years is painful, especially with two controlling, *let's do it my way*, type of women. And how many times have we heard that two women in a kitchen is one too many?

There were foods the girls and I missed eating. While shopping at the supermarket one day, Liz turned to me and said, "Look, Mom, Italian sausage. Wouldn't that be good for a change?" Italian sausage is something my girls and I loved to eat. But at my Jewish mother's house?

"I don't know, Liz, Grandma used to keep a Kosher home. I don't think she's ever eaten sausage in her life."

"Oh, please, Mom, please, we haven't had it in so long," Lizzie pleaded. The sausage went into the cart.

I love all kinds of sausage, something I developed a taste for when I discovered the joy of Italian food. My idea of a perfect sandwich, and one I imparted to my daughters, is Italian sausage on white bread with butter. This may sound disgusting, but it's kind of like the way non-Jews put mayonnaise on a pastrami sandwich. Anyway, Liz and Madi love this dish as much as I do. The first morning my mom and dad told us they would be gone for most of the day presented the opportunity for us to indulge. To be perfectly safe, we decided to have an early dinner. The sausage was sizzling in the pan when my parents walked in. From the way my mother reacted, you would have thought I was cooking her pet dog, even though she didn't have a dog.

"What is that smell?" my mom screamed. "And where is that smoke coming from?"

Always there to rescue me, Liz tried to explain, "Mom's making us dinner. We like sausage sandwiches."

"Sausage sandwiches? What kind of food is that? I can't believe you are ruining my frying pan and my kitchen." As she looked around the kitchen, the expression on my mom's face said it all. Having us there wasn't easy for her either. They were used to doing things the way they liked. I didn't know what to say.

"C'mon, Hy, let's go wait outside until this is over," my mother said, walking briskly toward the backyard, my father meekly following behind. I bet he would have loved a sausage sandwich but he was too afraid to ask for one. My mom might have killed him.

Somehow the sandwiches didn't taste as good as we anticipated. We didn't have sausage sandwiches again while living in Mom's house.

Another thing Mom hated was if I dared to change the station on her radio. Everything had to remain in place in her home. Now that I'm older, I can understand some of the things that were important to her, but at the time I was so stressed at trying to keep things together, it just aggravated me.

About a week after the sausage incident, Madi came home from school crying hysterically. "I hate it here and I'm not going back to that hateful school," she wailed. An hour later, when I helped myself to some liquid medication, my mother said, "Do you really need to have another drink?" That did it! I had to find a way back to the real world!

My boss was thrilled to hear I was returning to my job. Reservations were made. We were all at the airport, weeping excessively (except for Liz and Madi who couldn't wait to get back to Los Angeles), when the final blow was delivered. My mother sat me down in one of those uncomfortable airport chairs, staring into my hazel eyes with her brown ones. She had that ultra serious look on her face. I knew I would not enjoy this conversation.

"Listen, we've been generous in the past when Jack was sick, and we helped you out when you two divorced, but your father and I talked this over with your brother. You have to grow up and stand on your own two feet. You're a mother. We're not sending you any more money. You have to learn to be on your own." Then I *really* started to cry.

Chapter 3
Back to Los Angeles

My faithful friend Charlotte was waiting for us when we arrived at the Los Angeles airport. A few days before we left Connecticut I called her, moaning over my miserable circumstances. Being the kind soul she is, Charlotte offered to let us stay in her home while I looked for a house to rent. (Why do people constantly rescue me? I have no idea.) So there she was, all six feet of her, smiling as we got off the plane, eager to help pick up the luggage and drive us to Pasadena. I'm feeling no pain because I've got three drinks under my belt and it is barely two in the afternoon. The girls are quiet in the back seat, a sign they are worried about me. But they don't divulge the fact that men on the plane sent drinks over and one of them asked for my phone number.

The next day my friend Phil brought my car over to Charlotte's home. The girls loved Phil and were happy to see him. After a couple of hours I drove him back to his place. He told me he'd be around if I needed anything.

On Monday morning, the first thing I did was drive over to Glendale to register the girls for school. The administrator was pretty pissy, telling me they could not attend the school unless they lived in the Glendale School District. As she was talking, I feverishly tried to think of how I could get someone to lie and say we lived in Glendale. I needed an address but couldn't think of one person that would be willing to commit this crime. Instead, I called on my powers of persuasion and talked this unreasonable bureaucrat into giving me a couple of month's leeway, playing "the girls just lost their dad" card. She was not happy about this arrangement but when I turned on the tears, she gave in.

Now that the girls were going to school, my day started early in the morning. Charlotte lived about 15 minutes from downtown Los Angeles, but before I could drive to my office I drove the girls to their school in Glendale, which was in the opposite direction. After getting them up, we would all get dressed, have breakfast, prepare lunches, and then I drove to Glendale, dropped them off, and then drove another 40 minutes to Los Angeles.

Some people might not find all this driving burdensome but I was stressed out. Growing up in Manhattan, we didn't have a car until I was about twelve years old. Getting a driver's license and driving anywhere was not something I ever imagined doing. I could easily see myself as a Rockette, but I did not see myself as driving a motor vehicle. The way to get around in New York is to step off the curb, raise your hand and when a yellow vehicle arrives, you open the back door, jump in and tell the driver where to take you. It always worked for me until I moved to Los Angeles.

After I married Jack, before the girls were born, and before I had a car or a driver's license, I was so bored that I once hitchhiked to get to downtown Glendale. Downtown Glendale was kind of a joke. But even a poorly designed shopping center has appeal if you're stuck in an apartment for hours by yourself. That night, when I gleefully told Jack about my adventure, he became furious, forbidding me to ever hitchhike again, advising me of the pitfalls of taking rides from strangers. This was a new concept for me. All cab drivers were strangers.

Without transportation I was completely dependent on Jack, which I hated. Even though Jack was sick a lot of the time, he was the man of the house. In those days women did not have the power they have now. That doesn't mean I was a wimp. When he'd get home from work, I'm moan and groan, whining that I was bored, that I needed to get a job, I needed freedom. I would cry that I missed

New York. Poor Jack. He didn't want me to leave so he took me out driving whenever we had the time. But let's face it, driving never became my favorite thing to do. Each time I took the driving test I would fail, and we'd have a *crying jag weekend*. Before I knew it, we had two children and I still didn't have a driver's license. If I had to go somewhere when Jack was taking a nap and wouldn't get up, I would take the car and drive without a license, sometimes with the children in the car. I can't believe I did this but it's true.

Finally, when I was close to thirty, my mom told me she had obtained a driver's license at the ripe old age of fifty. How could my mother, who was older and shorter than me, get a license? I was determined to pass the driving test, even though I had failed so many times. Down to the Motor Vehicle Bureau we went on a Friday afternoon. At the end of the test, the instructor told me to park between two white lines. I was driving Jack's car, a long silver grey Cadillac. There was no way I could maneuver that huge vehicle between the lines. I'm only five feet tall and can barely see over the steering wheel! From his vantage point, Jack watched me try about five times. We both figured I failed the driving test again. It looked like it was going to be another horrible weekend for us. But, hey, miracles can happen!

Meekly, for me at least, I turned to the guy giving me the test, just about to say, "I guess I failed." For once, someone spoke before I did.

"Well," he stammered, "you passed but you really need to practice." Astounded, I said, "I passed? I passed? I passed?" Gleefully, I leapt out of the car, running toward Jack in my high heeled pumps. "I passed," I shouted, "I passed." An incredulous look on his face, Jack seized the moment, quickly walking over to the examiner, reaching out to shake the man's hand and patting him on the back with his other hand. The guy must have worried he'd made a mistake, or maybe he thought Jack was going to kiss him. Jack was beside himself with gratitude, saying to the thunderstruck man, "Thank you, thank you, sir. You have no idea how much this means to me." I knew what Jack was feeling. Relief! We wouldn't have the usual hysterical weekend with me crying, screaming and wishing I'd never left New York.

Summing up my driving life is simple. I hate to drive.

Driving my kids to Glendale, and then driving to my job in downtown Los Angeles every morning took over an hour. At night, I needed to drive to Glendale to pick them up, then back to Charlotte's house in Pasadena. It became obvious that it was time to make a move, not only because we needed to be in the appropriate school district, but we couldn't keep imposing on Charlotte and I could not keep driving back and forth.

During the time the three of us lived with Charlotte, who would not take any money from me, I was so grateful that I would often stop and buy groceries. I also bought her little gifts. I didn't know how to repay her. One morning when she took the girls to a pottery class, I washed the kitchen floor and cleaned all the kitchen cabinets. When she came home, she didn't say anything. I couldn't stand it. "Don't you notice anything?" I said.

Looking around, she replied, "No, should I?"

I felt like an unappreciated housewife, the same way I felt when Jack and I were married. I had to find a place for us to live, and in the right school district.

So, here's the deal. I had two weeks to find the right house. While frantically searching the ads for a rental, I was putting in at least 8 hours a day at the office, driving back and forth from Pasadena to Glendale to Los Angeles, helping the kids with homework and trying to stay out of Charlotte's way as much as possible. It had to be difficult for my wonderful friend to go from living alone to having two teenagers with their semi-hysterical mother living in her home.

Finally I found THE house! It was adorable. It was perfect. It had a pool. We moved in on a warm October day. The girls were ecstatic, immediately inviting friends for a pool party. I couldn't wait to tell the school we were finally legal. And then the bomb hit.

Chapter 4
The Wrong House

On Monday morning, with a big smile and a feeling of liberation, I drove the girls to school. They rushed to their classes while I went to the Administration Office. After waiting for twenty minutes (thank God there were no cell phones or my boss would have been calling me every ten minutes) I was led to the principal's office. Pleased with myself, I told her we'd moved.

"Where to?" she asked. Smugly, I gave her the address. I never saw this woman smile. Perhaps she had no teeth. And she was one of those very thin, emaciated women who look like they haven't had a decent meal in years. Her clothes looked handmade; she had obviously knitted the vest she was wearing. She hated me on sight. In the past she had dealt with Marilyn. So she knew the girls had not been living with me, which may have added to her unkind attitude. Who knew what Marilyn and Jack had told her.

Her slate gray eyes looked up at me, a smirk on her homely face. Then she actually smiled, but it looked more like a grimace. "Well, Mrs. Suarez, I'm sorry to tell you but that house is not in our school district."

My heart started to beat so fast I couldn't hear. "What did you say?" I asked, dumbfounded.

For a moment, I thought she was going to say, "Read my lips," but she had no sense of humor. No sense of compassion either. "I said that the address you've given me is in another school district. You will have to remove your children from the school and register them in your neighborhood."

"But we are in Glendale now," I reasoned. "We've moved out of Pasadena. I didn't know there was more than one school district in Glendale. It's not that big of a city."

With an icy stare she responded, "Mrs. Suarez, I've tried to work with you since Jack died, but you don't seem to listen or be able to focus on what the school district system is all about. You should have done some research. We have zoning rules. Can you understand that?"

I could not stand her condescending tone. The urge to stand up and punch her lights out almost overpowered me. But that would not solve anything. Besides, I'd never hit anyone in my life. Except my brother, until he got bigger than me.

Completely discouraged by her demeanor and exhausted by the schedule I was on, I looked at her without saying a word while I tried to compose my thoughts. What did she mean by "rules"? Those were not things I lived by. Never had. But now I was faced with a formidable force. I was sitting in front of a rigid, rule-abiding person who hated me on sight, a woman who had power over me. My mind went blank.

"Are you kidding?" I said, stalling for time and knowing this woman was incapable of kidding about anything. The thought of homicide crossed my mind, but what would it accomplish if I murdered her? Then my children would have no mother and no father. Not a good plan.

Defeated, I left her office, after agreeing to find suitable housing within a month. Where would I find the money to move again? Or the energy? I felt alone, angry, frustrated, and I was beginning to think the situation was hopeless. For one second I wondered if I should have stayed with my parents. Appalled at that idea, I thought harder, and did what I knew how to do. I called the man who had advised me to kidnap my own daughters, hoping he would rescue me one more time.

Chapter 5
The Right House

Even though we had not spoken all the time I was in Connecticut, he sounded happy to hear from me.

"Hi, I'm back from Connecticut. It didn't work out," I said.

Laughing, he said, "That's not a big surprise. You're hard to live with. You probably drove your parents crazy. The same way you drove me crazy. What do you need?" Always quick on the draw, he didn't beat around the bush. He was used to me coming to him for help.

"I need some cash."

"What happened to your family?" My family's wealth was a sore point with us because when we lived together, while we were having one of our many arguments, I'd told him I didn't need him or anyone, all I had to do was pick up the phone. Subsequently, he retaliated during another argument, saying, "I'm sick of you saying all you have to do is pick up the phone." There was this bit of tension between us, if you get my drift.

"They told me I have to grow up."

He laughed again, loving this situation. "Not a bad idea. It's about time. How much do you need? Where are you staying?"

"For a while we stayed with Charlotte. But for the last couple of weeks we've been living in a house I found that is in the wrong school district. I feel like I'm losing my mind."

There was a pause while each of us tried to guess what the other was thinking. We silently considered and discarded the idea of dating again. We'd been through too much pain to want to repeat the experience. We made plans to meet and he gave me the money I needed. Why didn't I swallow my pride and ask him back into my life? I could have used help. He was fun. He was smart. He was adorable to look at. And he was a great dancer. Lizzie and Madi loved him. I cared a lot for his beautiful two daughters. Looking back at that time, I'm pretty sure I could have talked him into giving me another chance. Instead, I thanked him, hugged him goodbye, got into my car and drove away. Another ill-fated decision that I regret.

Armed with a few bucks, I returned to my house hunting problem. The witch (spelled with a capital B) had given me an extension of one month, but only after I sobbed like a baby, ruining my makeup.

During that conversation, I thought of playing the *I'm-a-poor-widow* card but she knew I was only a grass widow. Instead, I just cried until she gave me the month.

There weren't many houses for rent in the appropriate school district, which I had marked off on a map in red pencil. After two days of following every lead, I was exhausted. Just when I thought it was an impossible dream, I found a house in the right Glendale school district. The house was a disaster, but when I met the agent at the property there was another couple considering it. Without looking closely but knowing it had three bedrooms and one bathroom, I said, "I'll take it. Where do I sign?" At this point, I was ready to rent a vacant lot, pitch a tent and build an outhouse if I could be in the right school district.

When I told Lizzie and Madi we were moving again they were incredulous. They loved their pool.

"I know you love the pool plus this house is ideal and has a lot of things we like. But we have no choice. I don't think you want to change schools instead."

In unison, they replied, "No, Mom, we can't change schools. All of our friends are in that school."

"Then we have to move. I'm sorry, believe me, this isn't easy on me either. You think I like packing and unpacking, moving from one place to another like a gypsy? I do have some good news though. The house I found has three bedrooms so you won't have to share a room anymore. Does that soften the blow?"

Having a space of their own had great appeal. One of the things they hated was sharing a bedroom. The other advantage was the new house was about three blocks from the house where they'd lived when Jack was still breathing, so they would be able to walk to school. After I pointed out the good aspects of the move, they accepted my decision. What else could they do? They were 12 and 13 years old. They couldn't book a ticket to Chicago. They were stuck with me and my choices.

Before we could move into the house in the right school district, it needed a ton of work. The walls were painted a putrid green so once again the man of the hour came to the rescue. Roger, a lovely man, painted most of the house by himself. Painting is something else I don't enjoy.

By this time you may be wondering exactly what did I enjoy doing at that time? Working and drinking are the two things that come to mind. The couple of times I helped Roger paint I wound up with more paint on me than the walls. After the house was painted and cleaned, I asked Zena and

Ronnie, my good very tall friends, to help me take the filthy curtains down. As Ronnie removed the lacy living room curtains they disintegrated. We laughed about this, had a couple of drinks, and I purchased inexpensive curtains to replace the ancient ones. The house was ready for occupancy.

After two weeks of packing again, moving again, calling the gas company, the electric company, having mail forwarded and all the other chores connected with moving, we were settled in. The girls were thrilled to be back in the old neighborhood where their friends lived. I no longer had to drive them to school, and they each had a bedroom of their own.

In less than four months we had moved from Glendale to Connecticut, moved in with Charlotte, chosen the right house in the wrong school district in Glendale, and finally found the right house in the right school district. Even writing about it is exhausting. Sheesh! No wonder I drank.

Chapter 6
The Red Tag Scandal

Things settled into a routine. In my never-ending resolve to be the perfect mother, I wanted to see my daughters off to school, making sure they had breakfast and I had time to pack them a good lunch. To accomplish this I changed my office hours so that I started work at 9:30. This meant I worked at least until 5:30 and oftentimes much later, leaving them on their own a lot of the time. Not a good idea for two teenagers with raging hormones, with no man in the house, and no one to keep an eye on them. Miraculously, they're both still alive and well.

One morning at about 10:15 I received a phone call at my office from one of the school administrators. "Mrs. Suarez, your children are not at school."

"That's impossible, Mrs. Jones, I saw them leave. I packed them a lunch. I know they are there."

There was a long pause. Then, in a stammering, awkward voice, she continued, "We hesitated about calling you but think you need to know. One of them called, trying to imitate your voice, saying they were being kept at home today." Laughing to myself, I thought how dumb could they be? I knew most of the administrators at the school. Plus my voice is unique because of severe asthma and the multitude of inhalers I use. And, I hate to admit, I smoked, causing more damage to my vocal cords.

"Oh," I said, stalling for time, my mind working frantically on how to handle this latest crisis. Where could they be? I started to panic. The area in which we lived was fairly safe. All the children in the neighborhood walked to school unless it was raining. Still, there were isolated cases of children being kidnapped, or maybe there had been an accident. Dozens of possible scenarios raced through my mind. Then sanity returned. I quickly dismissed all possible mishaps, knowing exactly where they were.

"Okay, thanks for calling. They will be at school in fifteen minutes. And, one more thing, can you red tag them so this won't happen again?"

"Yes, of course, we'll be happy to take more precautions. Thank you for caring."

"Of course I care! They are my daughters," I said. "Anyway, they'll be there soon."

Why did people seem to think that because I looked glamorous I didn't care about my girls? It was true that my appearance caused problems. The girls were embarrassed by the attention I received, especially in restaurants. But sometimes when we'd be snuggling in bed watching a movie, they would kiss me, say how beautiful they thought I was, and I knew they loved me as much as I loved them.

Instinctively, I knew they were at home. How should I deal with this situation? Why would they call the school? Instead of dwelling on why they went back home or wondering if there was a bad situation going on at school they had not divulged, I took action. One thing I had learned is that children watch their parents and scrutinize their every move. My daughters knew patience was not one of my virtues. Although I have many other character flaws, lack of patience is one of my worst failings. Liz and Madi had often seen me dial a number on the phone, let it ring three times and hang up. This drives people crazy. So when the phone rang three times at the house and stopped they knew it was me. They did not answer. When I called again and let the phone ring about 25 times, they knew it couldn't be me because I'd never last that long. They were wrong.

In a controlled voice, I asked, "Why are you home? This better be good."

Madi stammered around before answering. "We didn't want to go to school today."

"Why, are you sick?" That was another problem. When the girls would complain of a stomachache, headache, the usual, they got no sympathy from me. Living with a man who was sick all the time, and being sick myself, gave me no patience to deal with their being sick. I'd tell them to get up, take a shower and they'd be fine. Ah, such a loving mother. Anyway, Madi hemmed and hawed. I interrupted her feeble reasons for staying at home. No compassion, no further questions, I was the boss.

"Listen to me. The school is waiting for you. You are red tagged. If you're not there in fifteen minutes, the cops will be called. So get your asses in gear and run, don't walk, to school. They will call me when you arrive. And when you get home this afternoon, call me, and I'll call you back to make sure you're home. We'll deal with this tonight. Got it?"

"Yes, bye," she said, in a weak voice.

I was furious. For the rest of the day, I thought about how I would deal with this. Driving home in rush hour traffic, I wondered how I would ever get through these teenage years. Notice how I thought about myself first. Not "why did they feel they needed a day off? Are they having problems at school? Could something be going on they had not confided in me about?" Instead, all I could think about was what an inconvenience this was. In those days, it was all about me.

When I got home after six that evening the two of them were sitting on the edge of the bed in Lizzie's room watching television. Money wasn't flowing into the house so they shared a set. Without saying a word, I walked into Lizzie's room, turned off the television, and waved a hand for them to follow me into the living room. Fear was written on their faces.

"Sit down," I ordered, pointing to the frayed blue velveteen couch. They obeyed silently, no pushing, shoving, giggling. They knew they were in big trouble.

"Okay, I'm willing to listen. What went on this morning?"

Both of them started to speak. "One at a time. Liz, go first."

Looking upward as if God would give her the answer, she shrugged her slender shoulders. Then, those beautiful blue eyes cast down, she nervously replied, "We didn't feel like going to school today. It's boring."

"Boring? Boring? I'll tell you what's boring," I said, fuming. "Boring is when you stay home watching television all day. That's boring." Anyone who knows me understands that I despise television. For years, I tried to put the brakes on any television-watching in the house. Jack loved to watch television and we often fought about it. I'm a reader. I like books. So the thought of my daughters staying home all day watching television was repugnant to me. They sat there, silent.

"Plus you've been unfair. What did you do with the lunches I made you?" How could I bring up being fair? Was it fair their father died? Was it fair their mother worked all the time and thought more about herself than she did her children? Was it fair that Marilyn refused to give them back their furniture or any of the things that belonged to them?

"We ate them when we got back to the house," Madi said.

"Did you read the notes?" Every day I wrote each of them a short note that I included with their lunch. Years later, they confided to me how much they loved those notes. Liz said she would find a corner of the lunch yard to read hers. But I didn't know this at the time.

Each one nodded, indicating they'd read the notes. Looking at their despondent faces, for a moment I felt sorry for them. But that feeling of compassion didn't last. Then I went into my speech on what their behavior was doing to me. They were causing me to fail as a parent. Why didn't I have more sympathy? Ask them more questions?

The phone rang. I didn't answer it. I wasn't through with them.

"Okay, here's the deal. You are grounded for at least one month. You are red tagged at school. If you do this again, I'll be called immediately, which means I have to spend more time figuring out how to control things around here. That means time away from work, and it's my job that is keeping us together." As usual, always about me. How could I have been so stupid?

I continued, "Follow me," I said, angry, pissed off and disgusted with them.

They followed me into Lizzie's room and watched me unplug the television. Then they followed me into the garage and watched me place the television in the trunk of my car. Next were their clock radios.

"How will we get up in the morning?" they lamented.

"I'll wake you up."

Each school day for a month they came home, dutifully called me, and I called them back to ensure they were where they were at home. When I got home from a long day at work, we'd have dinner. No pizza for a month. But their homework was done. I took the time to go over every bit of it with them, and I felt I'd made the appropriate decision. I don't know now if I handled it the right way. It was a sad time for them and not one of my shining moments.

Chapter 7
Why Parents Go Deaf Before They're Thirty

Every once in a while my brain would focus on the fact that I was the full-time mother, the caretaker for these two teenagers. One afternoon I left work early, planning to spend some quality time and do something nice for them. When I was about two blocks from the house, I heard the music. As I got closer I became aware that the blaring noise was coming from our home. What can I say? All thoughts of doing something nice vanished.

By the time I pulled into the garage I imagined all of the flowers outside the house dancing to the beat of the music. What did anyone driving or walking by the house think? Why hadn't anyone reported this to the police? Fuming, I parked in the garage, opened the back door and walked through the laundry room toward the kitchen. The blaring sound at the other end of the house was deafening. The girls didn't realize I was home until I walked into the living room to turn off the stereo. The music was so loud I knew they would be deaf before they reached twenty years of age.

Immediately the house became quiet. With the stereo off the girls realized they were no longer alone. Sheepishly, they found me in the living room. Just as they walked in I glanced over to one of my favorite pieces of art, a detailed lithograph depicting the stock exchange in its early years, which hung over the stereo. Lo and behold, the large lithograph had slipped down because the reverberating sound of the music had loosened the glue.

Partly because I loved the lithograph and partly because I felt out of control, I walked into the kitchen, poured myself a scotch and soda, shaking my head as they followed me into the kitchen and watched me take a huge drink. For the rest of their lives, the sound of ice clinking in a glass would remind them of their mother's addiction to alcohol.

Taking another gulp of my drink, I looked at the two of them, and in a sarcastic tone of voice said, "You may not be deaf yet but you will be at an early age. When you need hearing aids you'll have to figure out how to pay for them yourselves. Why on earth do you play the music so loud?"

In unison, they replied, "I don't know."

"You don't know a lot of things, do you? Come sit on the couch." Walking as slowly as they could, they obeyed, knowing they were in for it again.

"You know what? Let me tell you something. I'm twenty-four years older than you, and I'll always be twenty-four years older than you." I continued, "And I'm smarter than you, and I'll always be smarter than you."

I was to give them this little speech many times over the years. Now I wonder how I had the audacity to repeatedly insult their intelligence and to believe what I was saying was funny. Some people think I have a great sense of humor, that I see the absurdity of life. That's true, but those years remain fixed in my mind as a constant and unfunny battle. I was trying to get them to behave as if they were thirty-five, or little robots; they were teenagers who needed love, compassion, gentle guidance and a nurturing parent. Instead, they had a self-centered woman more obsessed with her job and having a drink than being a responsible adult. It was a difficult time for all of us.

After I gave them this little bit of advice they looked at each other with tears in their eyes. Seeing how sad and frightened they were, I finally understood they were in pain. "C'mon, it's four o'clock. Why don't we straighten out the house and go out for pizza. Would you like that?"

You'd think I'd offered them a trip to Italy. Relief was written all over their beautiful faces. In that moment, the love I felt for them triumphed. I reached out my arms, asking for a hug. "I love you both," I said. "Life is just hard these days. Let's have fun tonight, okay?"

We had a blast. I let them order whatever they wanted, so they had cokes and pizza. We joked around. They were filled with stories of school, their friends, which teachers they liked and which teachers they hated. For one complete evening, I was there for them, listening, laughing, and nodding my head in understanding. When we got home, they got ready for bed, and each of them came into my room for a kiss goodnight. I've never forgotten that evening and I hope they also remember it with fondness.

Chapter 8
Born to Drive

During the next couple of years, I spent a lot of time at the school, worked long hours, drank a lot, and just tried to survive the trials of single motherhood.

When Lizzie was 14, she asked if she could have a slumber party. "Sure," I said, thinking it would be a lot of fun, something I never had when I was a teenager. My family had lived in a two-room tenement, two adults and three children. Occasionally I'd get to spend a night at my best friend's house, but slumber parties were not for ghetto dwellers like us.

The night of the big event arrived. Five 14-year-olds and Madi were there. The noise level was unbelievable, the giggling, the running around, the screaming. When Lizzie suggested I go out with my boyfriend to Churchill's, the local hangout place, we were eager to leave. Roger and I practically ran to his car and drove to Churchill's for a couple of hours, believing the girls were safe, having fun, making as much noise as they liked without us begging them to tone it down. I could picture them dancing in their nightgowns, happy to be teenagers. Talk about delusional!

About a month later, the truth came out.

You have to understand that Lizzie always said she was born to drive because her dad would hold her in his lap when she was a little girl, letting her pretend to drive his car. This was before rules about seatbelts, car seats, and safety devices.

One evening some weeks later, Liz found me in the kitchen. "Mom, I have to talk to you," she said.

"Okay, let's sit down in the living room."

She looked pale. Her blue eyes had tears in them. "What is it?" I asked, as we sat across from each other.

"Remember the night of the slumber party when you and Roger went to Churchill's?" Before I could answer, the front doorbell rang. Roger wasn't scheduled to drop by, but here he was.

"Come sit down, Roger," I said. Turning to Liz, I asked, "Is it okay if Roger hears what you have to say?"

Smiling, Liz said, "Sure. That would be fine."

Roger took the chair next to me so we were both facing Liz. Later, when I thought about our conversation, I figured Liz must have asked Roger to stop by because she must have thought I would strangle her.

"Yes, Lizzie, I remember. Roger and I were glad to leave you girls alone so you could play your music loudly." A little sarcasm thrown in.

"Well, Mom..." She hesitated, then glanced over at Roger. I turned toward him too and saw him nod in encouragement. "Well," she said again, quietly, "that night before you left I took your car keys out of your purse. After you went out to Churchill's, we all piled into your car and I drove us all around Glendale in your Cadillac."

I was stunned. Shocked. Out of my mind. A picture of Lizzie behind the wheel of my car, her friends screaming with delight, filled my mind. Then a picture of a terrible car crash appeared. My heart started to race. This time things were different; it wasn't rage that I felt. It was a deep fear that invaded my soul.

"I don't know what to say, Lizzie," I said quietly, terribly upset. Looking at my daughter's beautiful face, her lovely long hair, her blue, blue eyes with tears in them, I experienced a mother's worst nightmare. I could not stand the thought of anything happening to this child I loved so much.

"Listen, Lizzie," I said softly, tears streaming down my face. "I'm not going to punish you. I want you to know I love you and I'm scared. Do you know what would have happened if you'd had an accident and someone had been seriously injured?" Saying these words I could picture six slender teenagers lying on the street bleeding, maybe dead. Chills ran through me.

"No, Mom, I didn't think of an accident, I'm so sorry," she said, tears streaming down her face. "I don't know what would happen if we had a terrible accident," she sobbed.

"I'll tell you what could have happened, Lizzie. If there had been serious financial liability, we'd have to move. Like to Mexico. And my Spanish isn't that good." The attempt at humor fell flat.

She wiped her tears away, a mixture of emotions visible on her face. There was relief that she would not be punished. I could tell she was thinking of the ramifications of her actions. And I think I saw a glimmer of gratitude that she would not be grounded for the rest of her life. "I'm sorry, Mom, I really am."

"Lizzie, I believe you are," I said, trying to compose myself. With a deep sigh, I added, "So I'm willing to make an agreement with you. If you take driver education and don't steal my car or anyone else's again, I promise you that on your sixteenth birthday, no matter what it takes, I will buy you a car. Is that fair enough?"

Overwhelmed by the news that there would be no punishment, she looked at me, speechless, looked at Roger and merely nodded her assent. Later I learned that her conscience must have been bothering her because she first confessed her sin to Roger (or was she bragging? I'm still not sure). Anyway, he told her she needed to confess to her mother, which she decided to do. So there we were.

Standing up, she walked over to me, put her head on my shoulder and sobbed and sobbed. I sobbed too and the feeling of love I felt for her filled my body. Her hair smelled fresh, I could feel her tremble. And for a moment I was proud of the way I'd handled this unbelievable incident.

The next semester she dutifully attended driver education classes, then went to the Motor Vehicle Bureau to get her learner's permit. Roger was kind enough to take her out for driving practice. I was too chicken to take on that responsibility because I never felt comfortable driving. This was more about her safety than mine. Eventually I trusted she would not *borrow* my car and this became one more crisis we survived.

Chapter 9
The Dog from Hell

The girls just had to have a dog. They hounded me (pun intended) relentlessly. I argued with them for weeks, telling them we didn't need a dog, explaining that I'd wind up being the one responsible for the dog's care and I didn't have time. But they kept it up. Not a day passed when they did not mention our urgent need for a pet. Finally I caved.

A few days after I told them we could get a dog, while I was shopping in lovely downtown Glendale, I walked into a pet shop (why was I in a pet shop?) and, in my impulsive, not thinking way, bought a $300 Malamute with pedigree papers up the *ying-yang*.

Just what we needed! Why didn't I take the girls with me to the pound to choose a dog that would have cost a lot less? Why did I continue to make impulsive decisions that would greatly affect our lives without giving a moment's thought to what lay ahead? Where was my common sense? Instead of waiting and carefully considering what kind of dog to get, maybe doing a bit of research to see what kind of dog would fit in with our lifestyle, I see this cute, expensive puppy, charge the price of the dog and all the paraphernalia it needs on my credit card and drive it home. I am proud of myself when I bring this gorgeous dog home, knowing the girls will love him.

On the other hand, and to be fair to myself, part of the reason I didn't take them with me was because in my heart of hearts, I knew they would each choose a different dog, there would be a scene at the pound or pet shop, we'd all start screaming and I'd lose my temper, telling them, "No dog." They'd chalk it up to another broken promise. So I bought this expensive dog that I couldn't afford, a large Alaskan malamute. He was magnificent, with lush black and white fur, blue eyes and an intelligent face. Bright blue eyes, yes! Gorgeous, yes! Intelligent? Absolutely not!

Lizzie and Madi were ecstatic when they saw the puppy. Overjoyed, they promised to take care of him. They would feed him, walk him and bathe him. Right! They proclaimed I would never have to lift a finger to help train him, or feed him or do anything for him. And I believed them!

We sat in the living room watching him walk around on his large puppy paws, sniffing everything. And then we watched him pee. But we knew it was only a matter of time before he would understand that peeing was for outside. At least, that was the plan.

Then it was time to choose his name. Names flung out of all of our mouths. Cute names and silly names were tossed about. A magnificent looking creature like this needed a strong name. Because I was the only one in the family familiar with Shakespeare, I chose the name Brutus. At first, they said no, that was not a good name for their dog. But after going round and round for a few hours the girls could not come up with a name we all agreed on so Brutus it stayed.

Before I continue with this tale of woe, and to set the record straight, I love dogs. I like dogs better than I like people most of the time. But this dog had mental problems. Now that I've had time to analyze his behavior I think he might have been retarded. That is a definite possibility.

Madi, more than anyone else in the family, loved the dog. She spent hours chasing him around the small pond in the backyard, never tiring of throwing him a stick or a ball to catch. Now that Madi is grown up she still loves dogs, and always has one or two living with her.

After we'd had Brutus for a week or two, the girls called me at work. "Brutus is gone."

"Gone? How can he be gone?"

"He's not in the backyard. He must have jumped over the wall."

"How could he jump over a six foot wall? Someone must have stolen him out of the backyard." Wrong again. How could one person be wrong so many times? It amazes me that a successful woman, regarded as an intelligent being in the workforce, could lose all semblance of reasoning when dealing with teenagers and animals.

Not only could Brutus jump over a six foot wall, but that's exactly what he did. Just before I left work a couple of hours later, the girls called again. "He's at the pound. Someone telephoned. Will you get him on your way home from work?"

"Sure, I'll leave now. Thanks for letting me know." Driving home in the Los Angeles traffic, I began to wonder whether the dog had really jumped the wall or some passerby had let him out and then he got picked up by the pound. Could he really have been able to jump a wall that high? He was only a puppy.

When I picked him up, it was obvious he had jumped over the wall. His little paws were sore from landing on the sidewalk after taking that colossal jump. When I looked into his face, I felt sorry for him. Instead of walking him, I carried him out to the car, which was no easy task. I'm surprised I didn't slip a disk. Worn out from his adventure, he immediately fell asleep on the backseat.

This errant behavior continued. Each time he jumped the wall my sympathy level diminished. The pound got to know him well. They'd laugh when I picked him up. The dog was interfering with my life so much that during the day I'd wait for the phone to ring telling me the dog escaped again. I thought about leaving him locked in a bedroom, but he still wasn't housebroken. Even the girls were getting disgusted with his lack of good conduct.

Not willing to give up on him, I spent hours trying to train him. I'd take him out to the backyard, armed with treats in my pocket, in an attempt to teach him commands to come, to sit and to stay. But he just didn't get it. And we could *not* housebreak him. In order to make sure he did not poop in the house, we had to be vigilant about taking him outside. And the girls really paid attention. Even though he spent a good part of the day in the backyard, and Liz and Madi would take him out quite often, he preferred to relieve himself in the house. It was maddening.

Another one of his annoying traits manifested itself in the kitchen. Whenever I was at home, he followed me all over the house. Maybe he thought

I was in charge of treats. Or maybe he thought I was his mother. Or maybe he just didn't think.

Every time I'd go into the kitchen to get something, he was right behind me. If I opened the refrigerator, he'd walk right in. Not just get close to it to sniff a bit; that would have been okay. That would have been fairly normal behavior for a puppy. Brutus actually tried to climb into the refrigerator, putting his paws on top of the vegetable bin, trying to get at the food. One time he grabbed a piece of leftover chicken and ate it before I could stop him, plastic wrap and all. I was astounded!

He kept getting bigger and bigger and heavier and heavier. With his mind set on getting into the fridge, I'd have to pull him away, or scream for one of the girls to come and help me get him out of the fridge. By this time he weighed close to 80 pounds. The day he managed to get his two front paws into the refrigerator, enabling him to grab half a meatloaf I was planning to serve for dinner, was the day I began to hate the dog.

The bean bag chair episode was close to the last straw. The girls had to have a bean bag chair. It was an ugly, huge, brown, fake leather chair that I hated. But Brutus loved it. He loved it so much he ate it. Then he proceeded to poop bean bag stuff all over the place. The house was turning into a slum.

The fourth time he ended up at the pound, I thought about leaving him there forever...until Lizzie and Madi started to cry. Then I relented. But the finale occurred late one evening. I'd been out drinking, got home after midnight, took my high heels off so as not to wake the girls, and stepped in dog poop on the way to my bedroom. You can imagine having dog poop on your stockinged feet and how disgusting it would be to get rid of it. That was the climax to our worst experience as pet owners.

The next morning I told the girls the dog had to leave our happy home. Finally, after many tears, talks and pleading, the girls relented and agreed that the dog was taking up too much time and money, and causing too much aggravation. They said I could give Brutus to a co-worker who knew all about him. That day I told this young man he could pick up the dog that evening. When he showed up, I gave the eager young man the dog, his bowl, his food, his collar, his blanket and his pedigree papers, relieved to bring our ordeal to an end.

Ironically, within a few days, my co-worker told me that Brutus kept getting out of his yard and he'd given him to his mother. I never asked how his mother was dealing with the run-away dog. Maybe she had a higher wall in her backyard.

Chapter 10
Buying New Clothes

The girls were considerate about our financial position. They didn't ask for much and they understood we couldn't afford luxuries. Unfortunately, because I have no patience, taking them shopping for clothes turned out to be an unbearable ordeal. Jokes are often made about how much Jewish women love to shop. That might be true for a lot of women, Jewish or not, but it does not apply to my way of purchasing clothes, or anything else. When I need something, I make a trip to the store, look at a few items and make a quick choice. Not so with these two teenagers. Endless try-ons were accompanied with endless disputes.

I'd say, "That looks great, Liz, why don't we take that?" Or, "Gee, Madi, I love the way that looks on you."

"I hate this," Lizzie would say, dragging a few more items into the dressing room. And then Liz became obsessed with the size of her behind. This is how the shopping trip proceeded. First, Liz would look through the racks until she found a few items to try on. I would stand outside the dressing room waiting for her to appear. Frowning, she would come out wearing the item.

"How does this look?" she'd ask.

"Fine, fine," I'd say, unless it was atrocious. Then I'd just shake my head, no need for an involved discussion.

If she was considering the item, she would turn around, her back toward me, and twisting her head so she could watch my expression, she would ask, "How does the back look? Does my behind look huge?"

What could I say? She was fourteen. She had no idea what a huge behind looked like. I dreaded her asking me this question. Eventually it became hilarious. I finally reached the point where I'd offer to take a Polaroid picture of her behind so she could see that it wasn't anything to worry about. But it wasn't so funny when we were choosing clothes. I felt as if I had entered an insane asylum but I didn't know who the inmates were.

Then there was Madi, who would give me a look of disgust if I said anything looked good on her. She would roll her eyes, saying, "How can you say this looks good on me? I look like a dork."

One of the variables promoting this behavior was something of which I was unaware. What I didn't know was that the popular girls in school were called "soches." I'm not even sure how to spell the word. My daughters were worried about what these snobbish young girls would think of their clothes. So we weren't buying clothes that necessarily looked good on them, they were searching for items the other kids would think were cool.

These shopping expeditions became dreaded experiences. Had I behaved this way when my mom took me shopping? The only thing I remembered about getting new clothes was that my mom would go shopping alone, bring home a bunch of stuff and let me keep what I liked. Was it possible that my mom couldn't stand shopping with me for some of the same reasons? Hmmm. Something to think about.

Anyway, when it was necessary to add new clothes to their wardrobes, I hoped their attitude would change and we would have fun. But things only got worse as they got older. Here I was wearing tailored suits to work, trying to figure out what teenagers should wear. Fashion was changing rapidly. I couldn't keep up. On top of that, Los Angeles was at least three years behind what people were wearing in New York, which resulted in bizarre clothing combinations. I remember kids wearing leg warmers in 80-degree temperatures!

They needed to shop for clothes twice a year. Finally, I thought of a solution.

"I have a great idea," I said the next time school clothes were on the agenda. "How about I give you my credit card, drop you off at the mall and you go shopping without me? I'll tell you how much you can spend."

They loved this idea; they were thrilled. They never spent a dime more than the allotted allowance. When they were through shopping, they'd give me a call and I'd pick them up.

There is no need to discuss what I thought about their choices. I did not care if they wore striped blouses with plaid pants. The relief of not having to spend hours watching them try on the worst clothes ever made was worth it. I knew they would eventually develop their own sense of style. And they did.

Chapter 11
The Good Doctor

My lifestyle when the girls were growing up was not conducive to good health. My drinking was a large part of the problem. In addition, and this is hard to believe, I smoked. Smoking is the most treacherous thing with which an asthmatic can burden her respiratory system. In fact, it is one of the stupidest, most irresponsible decisions for someone with a history of pulmonary problems to make. There were many times when I'd stop smoking because it made me wheeze, cough and feel as if I might pass out. But drinking and smoking have a tendency to go hand in hand. Having a drink or two or three causes most inhibitions to vanish.

Because I smoked, the asthma was uncontrollable. No big surprise. So I went to see Dr. Dieterich, who was highly recommended as the best allergy doctor in Glendale. This was a relationship that would last for a long time. For the many years I was under his care, this wonderful doctor was continually kind to me. Unless he had no sense of smell, he must have known I smoked, but instead of asking if I smoked or telling me not to, he and I pretended it was not an issue.

He wasn't a very tall man. But as I recall the many times I went to him, coughing and wheezing, in my estimation he stands as a giant among many of the doctors I've seen through the years. Although he looked stern, with his full head of white hair, shining blue eyes and a serious expression on his face at all times, beneath that professional exterior was a gentleness of spirit. I knew he liked me and sincerely wanted to help me overcome this serious malady. Thinking back to those years, I realize he was a true gentleman from the old school, a man who respected his patients.

On my first visit to his office, he asked a lot of questions. When the question of smoking came up, I lied. To begin with, he tested me for allergies. After a series of allergy shots I noticed some improvement. Maybe if I had stopped smoking and listened to his recommendations, there would have been greater improvement, but I failed to take it seriously, believing I was immortal. What in the world was I thinking?

Whenever I caught a cold things turned nasty. I would cough so much my ribs hurt. Sleep was impossible. Instead of going to see Dr. Dieterich right away I would wait, optimistic that the cold would go away by itself. As the coughing continued, Liz or Madi would say something like, "Mom, you're not breathing right. Please go see the doctor."

By the time I made it to his office, I'd be in the throes of acute bronchitis, causing great distress to my respiratory system. The doctor would administer a shot of adrenalin, have me inhale oxygen, and prescribe large doses of prednisone. By the time I left his office I was trembling from the medication. But did that stop me from going to work, working all day, and then coming home to have dinner with the girls? No. I ignored my health. The temporary relief to my breathing enabled me to carry on. And instead of making it an early night, I'd often go out drinking and smoking until all hours of the morning. Naturally, the meds didn't do much good. I'd be back in his office either the next day or a day later.

Then one day Dr. Dieterich said, "Listen, why don't I inspect your home; maybe you're allergic to something there." I was allergic to my lifestyle, but I didn't want to bring it out in the open. I was content with the game he and I were playing where he didn't ask if I smoked and I didn't acknowledge my addiction. Instead, I went along with his suggestion.

"Okay, when will you be there?"

"How about Thursday?"

"Sounds good to me; I'll meet you there about one in the afternoon."

On Tuesday, I told the girls, "Please pick up your rooms. My allergy doctor will be here Thursday to see if I'm allergic to anything in the house."

Usually the girls didn't bother to hang up their clothes, and they never made their beds unless I forced them to do laundry and change the sheets. Makeup and other stuff littered their rooms. Once in a while, I'd get angry and tell them they had to clean up the mess, but it didn't take long until things reverted to their natural state, and I was too exhausted to care. The way I handled it was to close the door to their rooms. If I didn't see it, it wasn't there.

Having given them my instructions, I didn't think about it again until Thursday when I left work and rushed home to meet the good doctor. He arrived a few minutes after I did. First, he wanted to inspect the outside of the house. Taking notes, he pointed out some shrubbery that could be a problem, as we made our way through the backyard. The front yard was filled with beautiful flowers that Roger and Madi had planted. Fortunately, the doctor said they could stay. After our tour of the outside, we walked into the house. From the living room, we walked into my bedroom which was spotless, the bed was made, no clothing on the floor. I'm pretty neat most of the time. Lizzie's room looked good, too. I was impressed. And then we hit Madi's room.

"Who lives here?" Dr. Dieterich asked, raising his bushy white eyebrows.

Even so many years later I remember how I felt upon seeing her room. It's a miracle I didn't die of shame. Her room looked like a crazy person lived there. The bedspread was on the floor. Half of the sheets were off, leaving the mattress exposed. Shoes, socks, underwear and clothing covered the floor. In the middle of the messed up bed sat our Irish setter, Charlie, who had replaced the malamute, acting as if he lived there and wondering why were we disturbing him. If I'd thought faster, I could have said, "Oh, this is the dog's room."

Maybe she forgot or maybe she was getting revenge. I don't know, but it was a mess. What could I do? I drove back to my office, distraught, never focusing on the fact that I should have reminded her that morning that she needed to clean up her room. I should also have asked her what was going on in her life, and I should have been a better mother.

Pictures Through the Years

Me, wearing the silver chapeau, with Liz and Madi
(before washing machine fiasco)

Liz and Madi wearing coats made by Aunt Bessie

Madi and the Malamute, Brutus

Madi at the park, laughing

Madi laughing in pink sweater

My parents, Hy and Tillie Goldberg

Madi with her Grandfather

Liz and Madi playing cards at the Park

Acting silly about cigarettes

Good Friends Zena and Ronnie

Liz and Madi at Christmas

Liz attends Junior Prom

Liz with her younger children, Meital and Shahar

Liz and her
oldest daughter, Jacqui

Madi at swimming pool

Liz at swimming pool

Posing beside the black Cadillac

Charlotte and Madi, night of the kidnapping

At Connecticut airport

Madi and Liz at Mom's house

Mom, Lisa and Dad before Lisa's wedding

Leaving Connecticut with Mel saying goodbye

My Brother, Mel, with the girls at airport

My brother Mel, Madi and me

Arlene (Goldberg) Suarez aka Alexis Powers

All dressed up

Madi wearing my plaid hat

Liz wearing my plaid hat

Madi's school picture

Glamorous Madi playing dress-up

Newspaper clipping showing Liz as Homecoming Queen

Fur collar leather coat Mom bought me

Thoughtful moment in wide-brimmed hat

Lafayette Park Place apartment

Book signing at Barnes & Noble, Pasadena

Book signing for Kiss Daddy Goodbye

Book signing for Madi's Dollhouse.
Alexis with Connie, the Madi Doll maker

Book signing for Madi's Dollhouse

My Sister, Lisa, with Liz at Norton Simon Museum

Girls not happy at the Los Angeles Museum

Publicity shot for first book, Kiss My Tattoo

Mel and Sally in Aventura, Florida

My sister, Lisa, and her husband, Jon.

Mom, Sally and Elizabeth, the caretaker

Chapter 12
The Great Sun Roof Caper

At one point my daughters each found jobs at the mall. Amazing! I was delighted. Maybe they could pay for some of the things they needed, and they would learn how hard it was to make a buck. One fine day, even though Lizzie only had her learner's permit, she begged to use my car to take Madi to work. I relented, one more time. Another big mistake in a never-ending series of bad decisions.

They'd only been gone about ten minutes when the two of them walked back into the house, convulsed in laughter, rolling over with glee, giggling uncontrollably. This could only mean trouble.

"What happened?" I asked, unable to keep from laughing myself. That's because I was unaware of why they were so hysterical. Their attempt to explain was obscured by shrieks of amusement. Madi fell onto the couch, holding her stomach.

"C'mon, what happened? Am I going to think this is funny, too?"

Even in their advanced state of euphoria, they both shook their heads. I wasn't going to think this was funny. Finally, after what seemed like an hour, Liz squeaked out, "It was an accident." How many times had I heard this explanation? How many mothers have felt this sense of despair, dreading the news to follow?

"Okay, I understand. We all have accidents. Did you hit another car?" They found this statement uproarious. In my mind, I could see our car insurance rate going up into the stratosphere. I continued my interrogation. "Did you run someone over?" Even funnier!

"Okay, did you hit a dog or something?" Watching them laugh so hard, their faces contorted with glee, was entertaining. But I knew the finale would not be something where I got up and applauded.

"No, no, nothing like that," Lizzie managed.

"Please tell me what happened. The suspense is killing me."

Taking a deep breath, Madi sat on the couch and started to explain. "Lizzie was driving, and I was hot." More sidesplitting laugher. "So I opened the sun roof to get some air." Another long pause. "And then I don't know how it happened but the sun roof blew off the car."

The *I don't know how it happened* remark did two things. First, it put them over the moon. They fell down, laughing out of control. The second thing was it sent me into orbit wondering what the consequences of this *accident* were. While they sat there laughing their silly heads off, I rolled my eyes (something I often did when dealing with them), trying not to panic before I ventured to ask, "Yes, so what happened next? Did the sun roof blow off and kill someone?"

Totally amused, both of them said at the same time, "No, that's not it," followed by gales of laughter.

"What is it?"

Liz was laughing so hard she could not speak so Madi again tried to explain. "We pulled over because the sun roof was lying on the sidewalk. And it looked like it wasn't broken. So we were happy."

"But you're no longer happy, is that it?"

The laughter stopped. Looking at my serious expression they knew the time for frivolity had ended. Sad looks replaced their smiles.

When I remember that day, I wish I could have laughed with them. I could have said, "Hey, accidents happen." I could have said, "No big deal, I'll get it fixed."

Instead, I felt compelled to act like the strict mother. Maybe because I always felt so insecure about being the *perfect* parent, I failed to make the right decision. On the other hand, maybe I handled it the right way. I'll never know. What I do know is that instead of being kind to them, or making a joke out of it, I didn't. Instead, with the most serious look on my face I could muster, I said, "Well, this time I can't ignore your irresponsible behavior. There is no way I can drive the car to work and park it all day without the sun roof. I'll have to take tomorrow off from work to get it replaced. And this time you're going to pay me back for my expense."

Now, when we talk about this incident, we all laugh, remembering it as a humorous anecdote. They still think it was hilarious and they don't mention having to pay for the sun roof. I don't remember if they ever came up with the money to pay for it. None of that matters. The fun for them was watching the sun roof fly over their heads to land on the sidewalk.

Months ago, when I told them I was writing a memoir and asked them if they remembered anything funny from their childhood the first thing Madi mentioned was the sun roof. Liz also remembers the incident as a comical happening. Even though the incident happened over thirty years ago, they each remember it as one of their most fun experiences. Just hearing the words "sun roof" causes them to laugh.

Chapter 13
Sweet Sixteen Soiree

If you believe you create your own environment, I created a lot of remarkable circumstances in my lifetime, especially during my drinking years. For example, how many people go out for dinner, love the food, love the restaurant, and say to the server, "My compliments to the chef," before proceeding to leave the restaurant? That doesn't seem like out of the ordinary behavior, does it? The situation becomes out of the ordinary when the chef comes out to the table, chats with me and my date, and elaborates on how thrilled he is that we enjoyed our meal. That is the moment we went from out of the ordinary to off the planet. As I looked into his excited face, a brainstorm occurred and I asked him for his phone number.

After giving my outrageous idea some thought, probably for fifteen minutes or so a day for a few days, I called the chef. I explained to him that my younger daughter, Madi, was going to be sixteen years old in a couple of months. Could he come to the house and prepare a meal for our guests?

Where did I get the nerve to ask him? Where did I get the nerve to do so many crazy things? I didn't imagine he would agree, especially for what I was willing to pay. Once again, banishing any thought of being practical, I jumped into the arena. To my surprise and delight, after asking a couple of questions, such as how many guests we expected to attend, he accepted and we set a price. (He must really have needed the money!) So I began planning for the infamous Sweet Sixteen Soiree.

Invitations were sent out. Decorations were purchased. Each time I talked to the chef about what we would serve he assured me not to worry, emphasizing that he had some wonderful recipes. I suggested we do a buffet because of the large number of guests but he reacted as if I suggested we all go to Wendy's. "Finger foods are the way to go," he emphatically replied.

"Finger foods?" I asked, adding, "Will that be enough food for my guests?" When he said finger foods, I pictured cheese on crackers.

Over the phone I heard him sigh. "There will be plenty of food. Believe me, your guests will not leave your home hungry. Just leave the food selection in my hands. This will be a night to remember." I hate when people say things like that but I went along with him.

As we approached the date of the shindig, I called him to confirm everything was going along smoothly. During that phone call, the chef told me he doesn't drive! This did not make me happy, but I agreed to take him where he needed to go to buy the food for the celebration. He and I knew it was too late to make other arrangements.

So on the Friday before the big bash, there I was, driving from Glendale to Hollywood where he lived, then down to Chinatown located near downtown Los Angeles. We left the car in a parking lot and proceeded to walk up and down the crowded streets, buying things I would never dream of eating.

With complete focus, he inspected ducks hanging in storefronts. The ducks looked filthy to me, with hordes of flies buzzing around them but, as my stomach turned, he chose three. The guy wrapped them in old newspapers. I paid for them, praying that my guests would live through this culinary experience.

We approached a market where fresh fish were piled up on ice, their sightless eyes gazing up at us. I can't believe how carefully he inspected each dead fish, choosing six of them. More wrapping with old newspaper. He carried the bag. I imagined bad smells coming from the package. The thought entered my head that I was not imagining these whiffs of unpleasant aromas.

We walked down a street filled with Asian shoppers, different dialects filled the air, excitement all around, and I realized I was in a different world. I noticed that Chinatown had grown from the time I moved there many years ago. Most of my visits to Chinatown had been for dinner. There were several terrific Chinese restaurants to choose from. Interspersed with the Chinese restaurants were souvenir shops catering to visitors. The small stores featured silk slippers from China, beautiful paper fans, chopsticks and a colorful assortment of unusual items. During the day the area turned into a shopping area for the many Asians living in Los Angeles.

At the produce market he continued to touch, smell, and choose foreign looking items for which I paid. Many of his choices made me wish I had a few rabbits at home; the stuff sure didn't look edible to me. But, hey, what could I do? I'd made a decision, we were buying enough food to feed the Russian army and even though I was a bit apprehensive, I was excited. Smiling to myself, I noted that I was carrying a bag filled with additional bad smelling purchases. Again I wondered what I had gotten myself into.

After shopping for almost three hours, my feet hurt and I was exhausted. I was overheated, nervous and beginning to thoroughly regret this decision. By the time we got to my car and filled the trunk with our purchases I couldn't believe how much food we'd acquired or how much money I'd spent. My arms ached from carrying the packages.

All I wanted to do was take the chef home, drive back to my house and take a nap. As soon as I started the car he told me we were not through. He insisted that we drive to my home first so he could properly store the stuff in my refrigerator because he didn't have room in his small apartment. We didn't talk much on the ride from Chinatown to Glendale. My head was reeling at what a stupid thing I'd done.

It took us two trips to move the purchases from the trunk to the kitchen. Carefully, he arranged all this stuff on the counter. He had some kind of secret system for putting the food in the fridge. As I watched him, I was dying to have a drink. But I couldn't drink if I was driving him back to Hollywood. Instead, I had a diet soda. He asked for a glass of water. When we were finally finished, the refrigerator was overflowing. I would not be able to add an additional thing, not even an apple. Thank God the malamute didn't live here anymore.

Worn out, we got back into my car and I drove for another forty minutes to his apartment in Hollywood. On the way to his place he informed me that we had to shop early the next day, the day of the party, for the fish that had to stay alive until he was ready to cook. I was aghast when I heard this bad news but I didn't scream at him, "Are you crazy?" which is what I was thinking. It was way too late to turn back now. Just before he said goodbye, he instructed me to shower in the morning and to tell the girls they needed to shower before we got back because he would need to put the live lobsters in the bathtub when we returned to the house. Oh my God! Live Lobsters! How much would these cost!

I was at his house before nine the next morning. With an eager expression on his face, he was standing in front of his apartment building. Off we went.

This time we drove to little Tokyo where we parked in a more expensive parking lot. Once again I noticed hordes of Asian people food shopping. As we walked down the crowded streets, I saw tanks of live fish in the shops. He carefully chose several strange looking fish. This time the proprietor filled a plastic bag with water so the fish could stay alive. I felt like a kid buying a goldfish for a small fish bowl.

When we arrived at the store selling lobsters I was amazed at the selection. It looked like hundreds of lobsters crawling over each other. For a moment I felt sorry for these trapped creatures. With great intensity, the chef scrutinized the lobsters in all of the tanks, going back and forth, as I watched the people shopping. When he got the owner's attention, he chose two lobsters from one tank and one from another. The owner stated a price. The chef shook his head. By this time I was so sick of shopping I was willing to pay anything he asked for the lobsters, but the chef continued to bicker with the man in charge. Finally they agreed on a price. I pulled out my credit card. The three lobsters were placed into a large bag, rubber bands around their claws. On the way back to my house, the chef explained that the lobsters could live without water for a short period of time. As I mentally tallied up what I'd spent in the last two days, I realized I might have to float a loan. Or sell something like my diamond wedding ring. Or work two thousand hours of overtime.

Driving toward Glendale, I had this horrible vision of the lobsters pulling off their rubber bands, getting out of the bag, crawling toward the front seat and grabbing hold of my arm while I was driving. I realized I was beginning to hallucinate.

The girls were excited by all the food in the house, in the refrigerator and in the bathtub. They were exuberant, giggling and talking as they spent time on their hair and makeup before putting on their new dresses. They'd invited several of their friends and they wanted them to see what kind of a Bohemian their mother was. By six o'clock, the three of us looked beautiful, we'd spent hours on hair and make-up and we were more than ready for this gala event. I fixed myself a second scotch and soda to face the evening.

While we were driving around, the chef asked me if it was okay if he brought an assistant. Before I could ask how much this was going to cost, he explained that because the assistant recently graduated from culinary school and needed the practice, there would be no extra charge.

"Sure, bring an assistant as long as I don't have to pick him up." And as long as I don't have to give him any money, I thought.

"No," he assured me, smiling as if he was giving me a gift, "he has a car. He will pick me up so you won't have to drive to my place."

The fact that I did not have to pick up the chef before the anticipated event was a gift. Now I could start drinking at four in the afternoon.

At five minutes after six the doorbell rang. There stood the American chef with two Asian men behind him. All three of them were dressed in white jackets. They looked professional. The chef and I exchanged greetings. The assistants said nothing but bowed to me. It soon became apparent they spoke no English. I shuddered to think about how they'd gotten a driver's license. Maybe they didn't have a license? I didn't care. They were here. I thought I was having an anxiety attack. "Do you need anything?" I asked, walking toward the bar set up in the dining room.

"I need to know where your pots and pans are kept," the chef said, following closely, "and then you can leave us alone in the kitchen to prepare the food."

As per his instructions, I walked out of the kitchen, closing the door behind me. I was happy not to have to watch them deal with the dead fish, the live fish, the strange smelling vegetables and the lobsters. "Go to it," I said with bravado as I walked back into the living room, took a seat and enjoyed my drink before the party began.

The doorbell rang as the guests arrived. Drinks were served. The Suarez residence was famous for a good choice of alcoholic beverages but some guests preferred to bring their drink of choice. Conversation flowed and the house was filled with laughter. Before the guests could start on their second drink, platters of food were brought into the dining and living rooms by the assistants.

The serving dishes contained delicacies none of my guests or I had ever before tasted. The dishes were beautifully presented. The food was beyond delicious, the tempting choices filling the house with exotic aromas. My guests were swooning with delight, greatly enthused, nudging each other to try this or that. Dish after dish came from the kitchen to entice my guests with dazzling arrays of delectable bite-sized treats. From fish to duck the results were exquisite. I was amazed at how they had created these culinary delights from the hodge-podge of food we purchased. Each time I tasted something new, I was overwhelmed. My guests were eating more than they were drinking, a rare occurrence.

At ten I brought out the cake. We sang Happy Birthday. More food arrived. We ate until after eleven, when my guests started to say goodnight. By the time the chef and his assistants left and the guests were all gone, Liz, Madi and Lizzie's friend, Stacy, were all in bed. Without bothering to check the kitchen, I fell into bed, my stomach full. For a change, I had eaten more food than usual and was not drunk from too much alcohol.

Morning arrived. My stomach felt bloated from eating so much food the night before but it was worth the discomfort. I put on my robe and staggered into the bathroom, after which I moved toward the kitchen. Lizzie's friend, Stacy, emerged from one of the bedrooms at the same time. Together we walked through the dining room to push open the door to the kitchen.

"Oh, my God," I exclaimed.

Stacy, who came from a more religious background, said, "Holy Mother of God."

Every counter had something dirty on it. Every pan, pot, saucer, electric skillet, even cookie sheets and whatever else they could find to cook with had been used. I would swear that some of the pots didn't even belong to me. I did not remember ever using them for anything, much less ever seeing them in my kitchen. Even the tops of the washer and dryer had been used to cook with, holding two electric skillets coated with grease. My eyes rolled back into my head; I felt faint. Stacy grabbed my arm, "Are you okay?"

"No, I'm not. Let's board up the kitchen and move out. What do you think?"

Sweet child that she is, Stacy laughed and took my arm to lead me into the nightmare. "C'mon, let's dig in. I'll help you."

"I gotta have a cup of coffee first. Hang on."

The coffee pot was not sitting on the counter in its usual place. After searching for ten minutes, I found it tucked away on the floor of the laundry room. Stacy and I looked at each other, shrugging our shoulders. What else would I have trouble finding? While the coffee was brewing, we began to put the colossal mess in order, making up a system as we went along. And, miraculously, we made progress. Stacy was with me all the way.

After about two hours Lizzie and Madi emerged from their bedrooms. They offered to help, but after a few more hours, the girls had had enough. I didn't blame them. Grateful for their help, I whipped out a twenty dollar bill and told them to go to a movie. Off they went.

It took me two days to get my kitchen back in order.

No one ever forgot the party. The guests called to say what a great event it was. The girls talked about it for years. I vowed never to hire a chef again for the rest of my life. Unless he signed an agreement that he wouldn't leave the house until every dish, utensil and glass was washed and put away.

Chapter 14
Irons, Teachers, Onions and Laundry

Strange things often happened in our household. What would you think if you opened your refrigerator and found your iron sitting on a shelf? Would you be surprised? One morning when I opened the fridge to get milk for my coffee, there sat my iron. In my alcohol addled brain I thought it was a sign from the Almighty. The message was obvious; I should never iron again. When the cosmic universe delivers a loud and clear message, I obey my interpretation of what it means. I never ironed anything again.

Oddly enough, the universe was quite selective in delivering this edict. No one else believed what I thought the cosmic universe was saying. Other residents in our household loved to iron. Especially Lizzie. She ironed everything. I was afraid to rest my arm on the ironing board for fear it would be ironed by accident. One of her favorite things in the whole wide world was her iron.

Never love anything too much is my motto in life. Alas, one day a bad thing happened. The girls were at a slumber party. I was reading a book, in my flannel pajamas, enjoying a quiet evening at home. The doorbell rang and who to my wondering eyes should appear? Francie, who stands 5'9", has luxurious blonde hair, big brown eyes with long eyelashes, and a bone structure to die for. She's beautiful, witty, clever and fun. We are the dynamic duo.

She was ready to go out and frolic. "C'mon, the girls are gone. Let's have a drink at Churchill's," she suggested, although it was not really a suggestion. It was an order.

I put down my book and looked up at her. "Listen, Francie, I don't want to go out; I'm happy here. With Lizzie and Madi gone for the night, the house is quiet for a change and I can read."

Why did I bother trying to convince her I had no interest in going out? She should have been an actress. Out came an award winning performance by a minor actress in a minor role. With a sad look on her face she produced an imploring tone:

"Oh, please, c'mon on, let's go to Churchill's, Jimmy is working tonight."

Some women love movie stars, some women find television stars attractive, a few are fascinated by basketball players, but Francie loved bartenders. She couldn't get enough of these charismatic but usually impoverished creatures. That's why we hit the bars. She chit chats with them, flirts with them, tries to amuse them while I sit there, drinking, talking to the men who come by to see what's going on and buy us drinks.

"Okay, but just a couple of drinks. I have a busy day at work tomorrow."

"Great," she said, pleased she'd been able to convince me to leave my warm nest. She looked around the living room. "Do you have an iron?" she asked.

"No," I said, "but Lizzie does. She irons every day, kind of a fetish. Why?"

Looking down at her black skirt, she said, "My skirt is creased. I'll give it a quick go over before we leave. Okay?"

"Your skirt looks fine; it's black, it will get creased in the car. Wait here. I'll get dressed, be back in a few minutes." Why did she think anyone would notice a few creases in her skirt I wondered, as I went into the bathroom to put on that face everyone loved.

The house we were renting is a Spanish style built in 1929. Besides having a red tile roof and beautiful green tiles in the bathroom, it featured a built-in ironing board concealed behind a cabinet door in the kitchen. While I was busy dressing and getting ready for a night on the town, Francie occupied herself by pulling down the ironing board. She then found Lizzie's cherished iron. I was not aware of her activity in the kitchen until I heard a horrendous shriek. Terrified, thinking someone was killing her, I ran toward the kitchen. Francie was standing there in her white slip, holding up her skirt in one hand and the iron in her other hand.

"Shit," I said, "Lizzie is going to kill me."

"Kill you? What about my skirt?" The bottom of the iron was all black, completely covered with fabric. Francie's skirt now had a hole the same size and shape as the iron. We looked at each other and broke out laughing.

"We'd better get her an iron," I said, gasping for breath. And the next day we did. A brand new steam iron, so she forgave us our sin.

Early one evening I was in the kitchen fixing myself a drink. Madi walked in and said, "My teacher said you're an alcoholic."

"What?" I said. "What are you talking about? Why would she say a stupid thing like that?"

"One of the things we were talking about at school today was drinking. I raised my hand and said my mom has a drink every day when she comes home from work. She said you were an alcoholic."

"That's ridiculous," I responded. "Tell your teacher that if she had my job, she'd drink too." That was my excuse and the end of the conversation.

One morning I decided to make my famous homemade meat sauce to use for my lasagna recipe. Everyone loved it when I announced we're going to have lasagna for dinner. Making homemade sauce takes several hours to prepare but, hey, that's what mothers do, right? As I was in the kitchen organizing the necessary ingredients for my labor of love, the doorbell rang. It was my friend Mindy stopping in to say hello. Our home sometimes resembled Grand Central Station, with people dropping by unannounced.

"What's going on?" Mindy is adorable, a red haired, freckled, non-singing version of Bette Midler.

"Come in the kitchen. Liz is helping me make the sauce for the lasagna."

Mindy grabbed a cup out of the cupboard, poured herself some coffee, and then sat herself down in a chair to watch us get the sauce going. I handed Lizzie an onion.

"Here, Liz, this needs to be chopped."

"I hate to chop onions; it makes my eyes water," Lizzie half-heartedly complained. Mindy nodded her head in sympathy. She and Lizzie are kindred spirits.

"I know," I said.

Suddenly, as if she just remembered how to be a rocket scientist, Mindy jumped up out of her chair, excited, her red hair flying. "I know how to keep that from happening. My grandmother taught me a trick. Just stick a piece of bread in your mouth."

Instead of listening to this conversation, I concentrated on preparing the hamburger meat and sausage for cooking. Liz was at one counter, I was standing at another with our backs to each other, but I could hear the chopping of the onion. A few minutes passed, each of us engrossed in our tasks. At precisely the same moment we turned our heads so we were looking at each other. Liz was standing there with a slice of white bread sticking out of her mouth, tears streaming down her face from the onion. I totally lost it. We all started laughing. Liz dropped the bread on the floor when she opened her mouth to giggle. More wild hysteria. We never forgot that morning. No one ever again put a slice of bread in her mouth to stem tears caused by dicing onions. Except maybe Mindy.

One thing that mystifies me is hearing women rave about how doing laundry satisfies them. They go on and on about how they love the fresh smell of the clothes as they come out of the dryer. They enjoy folding the items and they feel productive when they put the newly washed clothes away. This feeling has never come over me. I feel productive when I get a bonus.

In fact, sometimes when Jack was sick, the children were small, and I felt completely overwhelmed with running the house, I would sneak the laundry off to Fluff and Fold. I never told anyone about this behavior. What would people think about a housewife who hates to do laundry? And another thing I wouldn't admit: I love the way my clothes look when they come out of the cleaners. Even if I liked to iron, I could never do a professional looking job. Another reason I was so happy to forget about ironing. That's what cleaners are for, aren't they?

Armed with this line of thinking, and absolutely hating to do laundry because it is so boring, I taught Lizzie and Madi at a young age to do their own laundry, rationalizing that it would make them feel grown up. Having this knowledge would prepare them to be adults. At least that was what I told myself. Sometimes they even offered to wash my clothes. And I let them. I'm not a stickler for everything being perfect because I've had some laundry disasters. One of the things that puzzles me the most is how many times I have put a completely, and I mean *completely,* white load of laundry in and when it comes out, every piece of it is pink. How does this happen? Why does it happen? Does the God of Laundry hate me?

Anyway, the girls did a lot of the laundry. And I believed they were happy doing it. In retrospect, as I reflect on certain situations, there may have been some passive/aggressive behavior going on with Liz and Madi. I thought you had to be older to practice the art of seeking revenge, but perhaps not.

For instance, one of the things that wound up in the laundry was a shiny silver and black beret that I loved. It had a tassel coming down the side and I wore it quite often. One morning I could not find my adorable little chapeau. With sheepish looks on their faces, Liz admitted that this hat of mine *accidently* wound up in the washing machine. "Where is it?" I asked.

"I'll get it," she said, looking at Madi as she left the living room. When she returned, she was holding up what used to be a beautiful hat. It never regained its youthful flair, if you know what I mean.

Another laundry disaster had to do with my keys. One morning as I was getting ready to leave for work, I looked everywhere, to no avail. I was running all over the house, screaming, "Has anyone seen my keys? I'm going to be late."

Noticing my anxiety, Madi piped up with an explanation. "I think I know where they are," she said, gleefully skipping toward the laundry room. And, lo and behold, they were in the washer. Strange, isn't it?

Chapter 15
Driving Calamities

We've established that I hate to drive. The girls have heard me complain about driving since before they could talk. Because Lizzie was obsessed with wanting to drive, she offered to drive every time we needed to go somewhere. Although this was a kind offer, there existed a small problem. She did not have her driver's license because she wasn't yet sixteen. Liz did not view this minor obstacle as problematic.

Here is a bit of background into why I hate to drive. First, I lived in Manhattan until I was about 22. There is an enormous amount of public transportation available in New York City. The lack of a car is no obstacle to getting around the city. Trains and buses took me anywhere I had to go. If I was in a big hurry, I could wave down a taxi. When I started to work and had money in my pocket, taxis became a way of life. In my mind, if I needed to go somewhere I could stand in the street, wave my hand and a car with a driver would show up to whisk me away. I loved New York. I was fond of saying, "I will never move out of New York City. I love to travel and see the world, but New York City is my home."

Life happens and things change. My family finally got a car when I was about 12, but I still never thought about personally driving. Probably because my dad was not the best driver in the world, I felt safer in a taxi. Then, surprisingly, when I was 19, my dad advised me to take driving lessons. "You never know what will happen and you should at least have a license."

My father and I had a beautiful relationship. Although I never listened to any advice, occasionally I would do what my father asked because I loved him so much. So I took ten driving lessons in the city on my lunch hour in a dual controlled car. On the day of my driving test, as I was leaving our apartment, my dad handed me a folded $20 bill.

"What's that for?" I said.

"Just put it on the seat when you and the instructor get into the car. Then you'll pass the test." Now I knew how my dad got his driver's license.

I was indignant! "Are you kidding? Why would I do that? That is so dishonest. I can't believe you said that."

Who was it that said "Youth is wasted on the young"? I should have listened to my father. Right off the bat I knew I was failing this test because as we pulled away from the curb, I didn't see a car coming. Fortunately, we were in a dual controlled car and the instructor slammed on the brake. Sweat appeared on his forehead. If I had been the guy giving the test and that happened I would have taken control of the car and driven straight back to the Motor Vehicle Bureau, but he stuck it out. We went through the rest of the drill, but he didn't ask me to make a U-turn, which I knew was part of the exam and something I was dreading. I'm still not crazy about making U-turns, unless I'm driving on a football field.

"I guess I didn't pass," I said innocently when we were back at the Motor Vehicle Bureau.

Not even giving me a glance, just relieved to be getting out of the car, he said, "You'll be notified by mail." Being a naïve young woman, I foolishly thought there was a chance I passed. When the failure notice arrived, I cried. My dad was not sympathetic. "You never listen. You don't listen to me and you don't listen to your mom. What's wrong with you?"

I've heard these words uttered many times by many people throughout my life. But I pay them no heed. In my heart of hearts, I know there is nothing wrong with me. It's the other folks who don't get it.

As I said, things change. When I moved to southern California, got married and had children, it became apparent that I had to learn to drive. At that time public transportation in Los Angeles was a joke. Maybe it still is. Poor Jack. He was patient. He took me out driving whenever he had the time. Maybe that's one of the things that aggravated his heart condition, but he never complained. Finally, by some miracle, I got my driver's license when I was close to thirty years old. That is after failing the driving test about six times.

Back to my story about Lizzie's compulsion to drive. I told Lizzie for the hundredth time, "You can't drive. You don't have a license."

"Will you let me drive when I have my learner's permit?"

"Probably, but since you don't have a learner's permit there is no reason to have this discussion. You have to take your class in driver education before you can get the permit." That ended the conversation for the day.

Then there was the other irritating squabble that occurred whenever I had to take them somewhere or we were going on an outing. We would get to the car and I would unlock the door on the driver's side. The three of us would look at each other in expectation. We knew the drill and what was going to happen next. It never fails; they start arguing.

"I want to sit in front," Liz demanded.

"Well, I want to sit in front. You sat in front last time. It's my turn," Madi argued.

"I'm older," Lizzie reasoned. "I should sit in front." After a few minutes of listening to this obnoxious quarrel, I make the decision.

"No one sits in front. Both of you get in back." They don't like it but they have no choice. Off we go.

The girls had not learned to control their bodily functions, at least not when they were in a car with me driving. Maybe they did this to get on my nerves. When the smell hit the front seat, I immediately pushed the button to roll down all the windows. The occasion I remember most vividly did not happen on a warm day; in fact, it was pretty chilly for southern California, but I didn't care if there was a blizzard going on. I almost fainted from the odor. How could children of mine smell so bad? By the time fresh air entered the car, I was gagging. I was no longer driving the car with the sun roof; that one was long gone. My new car was a long, black Cadillac. I'm so short people ask me if I drive by looking through the steering wheel. Anyway, the windows went down, the laughter and hysteria went up. They found this extremely humorous; they didn't stop laughing for a long time. I wondered if I'd ever get through these teenage years.

Chapter 16
Born to Drive, Part Two

As I've mentioned before, when Lizzie was just a little girl Jack would sit her in his lap when driving. She would play with the steering wheel and make believe she was driving the car. As a result, she could not wait to drive. The closer we got to her 16th birthday, the more she started badgering me about wanting her own transportation. I hoped I would go deaf so I didn't have to hear her constant pestering.

"When can I get my car?"

"Look, Lizzie, I promised you a car, didn't I? I'll get it as close to your sixteenth birthday as possible. But you have to give me a break. Do you know that cars cost money?"

The rolling of the eyes. "Yes, I know that cars cost money, Mom, of course I know that. But you have money for everything you want, why can't I have a car? I'll be sixteen before you know it."

"You know, Lizzie, you drive me crazy. When you made up my budget a couple of months ago, you kind of left certain things out, such as food, car insurance, clothing for you and your sister, and a hundred other expenses you don't even know about. And the problem is not only getting you a car. There is a law that requires you have car insurance. Do you have any idea how much car insurance costs for teenagers?"

"Well, Mom," she whined, "you promised I could get a car."

"I'll do what I can, now please stop bugging me."

The months rolled by and we were quickly approaching March 9, the date of her birthday. Where could I get the money for a car? And she would not settle for just any car. She had her heart set on a 1964 Ford Mustang. That's all she talked about. Every kid her age wanted one of those. They were in high demand and my credit cards were pretty much maxed out.

Deep inside me, I knew part of what she said was true. There weren't too many things I deprived myself of. I loved clothes, I wore hats, and I was an impulsive buyer. On the other hand, I gave them an ample budget for clothes. They accompanied me to fancy restaurants, and even though we were usually with some guy who paid the check, they had the benefit of being out on the town. And I sometimes splurged. I was like the Federal government. Buy now, worry about it later.

Nevertheless, a car for Lizzie was different from buying a coat for two hundred bucks. The car she dreamed of driving would cost around $3,000, and car insurance for a sixteen year old was expensive. I would find out later why teenagers pay so much for car insurance.

Two days before her birthday, I made a decision. This time I turned to my brother.

"Hi, Mel, what's new?"

"Life is good. What do you need?" My brother knows me. I don't call him to chit-chat.

"Lizzie needs a car. She turns sixteen in two days."

"How much?" My brother doesn't go in for long conversations.

"Three thousand should cover it. I'll find a way to pay for the insurance."

"I'll throw a check in the mail this afternoon. Anything else?"

"No, Mel, thanks, you're wonderful."

"I know." And he was gone.

The car search began. Desire is the key to attainment. If someone perseveres to reach a goal, they will most often succeed. Nothing would stop Liz from finding the car she had thought about for months. She was thrilled at the idea of having her own wheels and she asked everyone she knew to help her find a 1964 Mustang. After a few leads that did not materialize, she finally found a yellow one.

We had someone who knew a lot about cars take a look. He gave his approval and we bought it. One day Lizzie got her driver's license. The next day the car was parked outside of our house. Liz had her own car. Nothing could be better. Now she was totally out of my control. The car changed our lives. No longer did I have to drive her anywhere and sometimes she was kind enough to take Madi where she needed to go. The car insurance was astronomical but I paid it. Now that Liz had a car, she drove herself to the job she had after school at the mall. In some ways it was a relief not to have to drive her. But I was uneasy. I worried. I didn't want anything bad to happen to her.

One evening as we were sitting in the living room, Liz said, "Mom, let me take you for a drive."

"No, I'm tired, Liz."

"Please, Mom, please, just around the block." How could I refuse this child I loved so much?

Nothing bad happened, but I hated riding with her. She scared me with how fast she drove. Despite my fear, I had to admit she was a better driver than I would ever be. She had a rhythm to her driving that I lacked. Maybe she was right when she said she was born to drive. She'd had a bicycle as a youngster, and I believe that people who never learn to ride a bike are not good drivers later in life. Obviously, I never learned to ride a bike.

One evening, Liz announced she was going to visit her cousin, Deanie, on the other side of Glendale. Madi begged to go along but Liz refused.

"C'mon, Liz," I said, "why don't you take your sister with you? She has no plans tonight."

Nothing we said could convince her to let Madi go with her.

"Don't worry, Madi," I said, "I'll take you out for pizza." My heart ached for Madi.

Looking disgusted, Liz said, "You're so mean to me, Mom! Just because I don't want to take that baby with me, you're going out for pizza. Well, go have pizza. See if I care." She left the house, slamming the door behind her. I took Madi out for pizza and we watched a little television together before we went to bed. About two in the morning the phone rang, waking me from a deep sleep. Immediately awake, with my heart racing, I answered the phone.

"Hello," I said, knowing this was bad news.

"Mom," Liz cried. "I need you."

And need me she did. I threw on some jeans and a sweatshirt, running to the garage where, with trembling hands, I started my car. On the way to pick her up, my mind envisioned horrible scenarios. On the phone, she'd said she had an accident but she swore she wasn't hurt. I didn't believe her.

Driving down the dark street, I saw her standing on the pavement, alone. The Mustang had been towed away. Although the police had offered to drive her home, she'd insisted that she would wait for her mother to pick her up. Even at her tender age, she had the ability to convince people to do things that did not make sense. So the police allowed her to stand there by herself at two in the morning to wait for me. She jumped in my car, sobbing.

"Are you sure you're not hurt?" I asked, sick to my stomach. She looked so small, so vulnerable. Tears streaked her beautiful face and her hair was plastered to her face from all the crying.

"No, Mom, I'm not hurt but the tow truck guy said my car is totaled."

My first thought was I was grateful she had not taken Madi with her but I didn't mention that. Instead, I said, "Don't cry, sweetheart, somehow I'll get you another car."

And I did.

Chapter 17
Raging Hormones

The girls were on their way to becoming women. The signs were all there: mood swings, erratic behavior, crying for no apparent reason, changed eating habits, and an obsession with how they looked. All of a sudden they noticed there was a difference between boys and girls. They no longer hated the male gender. They went from saying, "Yuck, boys," to saying things like, "Isn't he cute?" or "Do you think we'll see him today? And they whispered to each other, especially when I was driving them somewhere. And they giggled. Oh, how they giggled.

They needed instruction on how to behave around boys. At least, that was my take on the situation. One evening I came home, made dinner and began a conversation with them.

"Now that you're thinking of dating, we should have some discussion about boys, don't you think?

Gales of laughter. Not as bad as the sun roof frenzy but pretty darn close. "What's so funny?"

Liz responded between titters, "Oh, Mom, you're so old fashioned. We know how to talk to boys."

Hmmm, I thought, I bet, but I continued to act like *the mom.*

"Okay," I said, stalling for time, "here are some thoughts I have. If you go out with a young man, I want the boy to come in and introduce himself. We also have to set up time parameters so I don't sit up late worrying. Do you have any thoughts on this?"

More chuckles, and this time Madi piped up, "A young man?" For some reason, they found this reference very funny. I guess they did not realize they were emerging from their cocoons of childhood as young women.

The next one to remark was Liz, "Why don't you wait until we have a date to discuss this?"

"Because then it might be too late."

In unison: "Too late for what?"

"Obviously it is too late tonight for me to continue this conversation, but let me tell you one thing right now. This passing wind has to stop. Or you'll never have a date."

This caused them to go into spasms of hooting. They couldn't stop laughing which caused one of them to lose control and let go a loud one. They were beside themselves. I got up from the chair and stood in front of them. "Here is a demonstration of what you two look like."

I swung one hip out to the right and said, "boop, boop," mimicking their passing wind. Then I swung the other hip out, repeating these words. And then I swung my hips from side to side, saying, "boop, boop, boop." This put them totally into orbit. They fell off the couch they were laughing so hard. This was pretty entertaining, even to me.

"Trust me on this one, girls. If you don't learn to control your bodily functions, not only will you never have a date but there is no chance you will find someone willing to marry you." We went to our rooms laughing. Through the years, this has been a dispute about whether I was imitating them or they were imitating me. But this is my story and I'm sticking with it.

After dinner the next evening, I produced a form I'd created at my office. "Here, take a look at this. You can give this to any boy who asks you out for a date."

The form is droll humor, asking for the boy's name, what kind of car he drives, has he ever received a driving violation, what are his plans for the future, what his father does to provide for his family and whether his parents rent or own their home. After Lizzie and Madi read the form, they looked at each other, stalling for time. Then they looked at me, confused expressions on their faces. They never knew when I was being serious or playing with them.

Liz spoke first. "Mom, is this like a joke? Are we supposed to give this to someone who asks us on a date?"

Then Madi put her two cents in. "We can't do this, Mom. No one will ever take us out." We had another good laugh that evening.

The boys started calling and soon began dropping by. There was constant giggling. The girls were on the phone with their girlfriends all the time. I was gone most of the day and that had me worried. I'd told them the facts of life all through their growing up years, but could my practical advice compete against their hormonal desires?

After much thought, I came up with a way to find out more about what was going on, at least in school. I pursued friendships with their teachers. Most of them were standoffish, but Lizzie's English teacher and I hit it off. She was a few years younger than me but she understood exactly what my concerns were. I was grateful for her friendship and once in a while, on a Saturday, she and I would have lunch. Looking back, I think she realized the difficult time I was going through trying to control my teenagers at the same time I had to work to support them.

One afternoon she called me at the office to tell me that Lizzie was paying more attention to a boy in her class than she was to anything else.

"Oh," said I, "tell me more."

"The boy's name is Robert, but they call him Bobby."

"What does he look like?"

"Cute, dark hair, dark eyes, a little wild."

"Fifteen year old boys are either wild or boring, wouldn't you say?"

"Yes, I would," she laughed. "Just giving you some warning of what is going on."

"I appreciate it. Thanks."

After dinner a few days later the three of us were sitting in the living room. They were playing Chinese checkers and I was reading a book. Now was the time, I thought.

"Liz," I said, and they both looked up at me. "I had a dream last night, kind of when I was sleeping but slightly awake." I really had their attention now. I continued, "I don't know if I was really dreaming. It was sort of a message from somewhere in space."

This was something new. They stared at me, not knowing what to expect.

"Really," Liz said, in a sarcastic tone, "What message did you get?" There was a sardonic grin on her face. She was prepared to argue with me no matter what I came up with.

"This dream or vision was about you and some young man. I'm wondering if you are keeping something from me. Are you interested in some boy in your class?"

Raised eyebrows. This was not what she was expecting me to say. "No, Mom, are you serious?" I could tell by her expression she was not telling the truth. She never learned to lie. Not to this day.

"Yes, I'm very serious." I paused for effect. Both of them were staring at me as if I'd just landed in a spaceship. "Wait, be quiet," I said, "Let me concentrate on what the message was." They were transfixed, startled by this conversation.

I closed my eyes, raised my face to the ceiling, and pretended to be meditating. Not a sound, I don't even hear them breathing. By using extreme concentration, I don't break out laughing.

In a low modulated voice I said, "I see a young man...no, a boy, with dark hair, dark eyes."

Gasps from my attentive audience. I took a deep breath.

"And I think I see a name." Again I paused for effect but didn't look at them, keeping my eyes closed and praying I didn't blow my delivery. Slowly, as if the information was coming to me from some mystical place, I said, "His name, his name is Rob or Robbie, no . . . his name is Bobby. That's it!"

Slowly, I opened my eyes.

"Oh, my God!" Liz shouted, "What else do you see?"

Again, I closed my eyes. I had them where I wanted them. "Dark hair, I think it's curly, he has brown eyes, and I see danger there." It was difficult not to burst out laughing, but I was into the charade, loving my own Academy Award performance.

When I looked at Lizzie and Madi, their eyebrows were hitting their foreheads. They couldn't think of anything to say. I couldn't believe how cleverly I'd fooled them. They were shocked. Without a word, at the same precise moment, the two of them stood, then practically ran into Lizzie's room. They needed to discuss this alone to figure out how I had known.

Things changed after that. There was more respect in their attitude toward me. On several occasions, they'd quietly ask me to use my *physic* powers to tell them something they wanted to know. I'd go through the whole charade, close my eyes, pretend I was connecting to the spiritual universe and make up some appropriate response.

Not only were they astounded, they told their girlfriends about my amazing ability. They bought it hook, line and sinker. The English teacher and I had lunch and we laughed ourselves silly. I didn't tell my daughters the truth until a few years ago. Even though we don't talk about it, it's possible they may still wonder if their mother can "see things."

Chapter 18
A Boy Wearing a Dog Chain

One day there arrived in our world a boy, or a man or a crazy person, named Toby, Lizzie's idiot boyfriend who wore a dog chain instead of a gold chain. What can I say? No class. This boy (moron is a better word) drove me to the brink of homicide or suicide. Other than looking like he was recently released from a mental institution, he would call our house at two or three in the morning, waking me out of deep sleep because the phone was in my bedroom.

I begged Lizzie to tell him to stop calling in the middle of the night. I even had our phone number changed but she gave him the new number. This unbearable situation forced me to get Lizzie her own phone. And this was a long way before kids had their own cell phones, ipads, computers, etc.

No matter what I said or how hard I pleaded she would not stop dating this repulsive creature. This went on for months but it seemed like a thousand years. I would talk until there were no words left for me to say to her, but the relationship continued.

Two things eventually occurred that solved the problem.

First, when I left the house one day he was parked in the street in front of our house waiting to follow me to find Liz. We were helping a friend move and Liz was already there. I knew the traffic light system very well on the street where we lived. So I drove slowly, with him close behind, making sure I hit the light when it turned red. When the light turned green, I put the car in reverse, slammed into him, and then drove off. I didn't know he was driving his mother's car, but I doubt that would have changed my behavior. Sometimes when I think of this incident, I am ashamed of myself. He was just a silly kid and I was supposed to be a responsible adult. On the other hand, desperate situations cause people to take desperate action. I thought that would surely be the end of him. I was wrong.

Liz couldn't believe I had crashed backwards into his car. She was really upset. Then she tried to convince me to change my attitude towards this numbskull. "Mom, you have the wrong idea. Toby is a good guy, we love each other. Please give him a chance."

What could I say? I felt contrite about damaging his mother's car. I loved Lizzie, and I couldn't keep trying to make her do what I thought was right. So I took a giant leap of faith.

"Okay, Liz, why don't you and Toby join us Saturday night when Zena, Ronnie, Peter and I go to dinner? Would you like to do that? This way I can get to know him." Peter was the new man in my life.

She was thrilled. "Really, Mom, really? That would be wonderful," Liz said, coming over and giving me a big hug of gratitude.

Saturday night arrived. The four of us were having a drink at the bar waiting for our table when Liz and Toby showed up. He still wore the ridiculous dog chain but instead of a raggedy t-shirt he was wearing a "real" shirt, jeans, and had recently shaved. Liz looked gorgeous, dressed to the nines, wanting to impress my new boyfriend and my friends.

Our name was called and we were seated at a table. Food orders were taken, food was delivered, and conversation flowed. I don't remember exactly what we started discussing, probably books, films, politics, the usual.

And then the answer to my prayers occurred. Toby joined the conversation. We all looked at him, eager to hear what he had to say. He started talking, talking and talking. The five of us were mesmerized by his non-stop monologue; he would not shut up. And he spoke gibberish. He was unable to make a complete sentence. Whatever he was trying to convey came out garbled. We were polite adults, we listened, and we earnestly tried to understand what message he was delivering. Peter nudged me under the table but we were afraid to look at each other for fear of laughing at him. I glanced over at Ronnie and Zena who were both staring at the roll on their bread plates as if they'd never seen bread before, obviously embarrassed for this poor soul. Then I gazed over at my daughter. Lizzie was staring at this moronic individual, her eyes open wide, as if she had seen a spaceship land in the restaurant. Her cheeks were bright red. I wondered if she would get off her chair and hide under the table.

That turned out to be their last date. We never saw or heard from Toby again. I rested easy. But that relief only lasted for a while.

The next boyfriend on the scene was Frank, the handsome Italian stud. He was adorable, with dark curly hair, big brown eyes and a warm personality. Frank was a big improvement over Toby. Even if Lizzie started dating a gorilla it would have been an improvement over Toby.

Just before Christmas, Frank had his mother call to invite us to join them for dinner on Christmas

Eve. I said to Peter, "Growing up in New York we were surrounded by Italians. They are the best cooks in the world. We're going to have a fabulous dinner."

How could one person be so wrong so many times in life? To this day I've never met another Italian who could not prepare a decent meal. The evening was torturous as we valiantly ate the food set before us. When I was halfway through the meal, I wondered if we'd live to see another Christmas. The pasta was so overcooked it liquefied in my mouth. Sort of like a good red velvet cake. Except it wasn't good. The sauce had some unidentifiable ingredient in it that made me cough. I thought I'd have an asthma attack. By the time we left, Peter had a greenish tint to his face.

When we got home, Peter ran into the bathroom and threw up. Then he left, refusing my offer of either a cup of tea or a cup of coffee. I hoped he didn't drop dead from food poisoning. After he left, the three of us sat in the living room without talking. Liz was the first to react, "Oh my God," she said, "can you believe that meal?"

Laughing, Madi, Liz and I hit the kitchen, opened the refrigerator, and pulled out anything we could find to make ourselves sandwiches. I think I had tuna and the girls had peanut butter and jelly. Liz started to apologize for the agonizing meal, but as we started talking about each of the horrible dishes they had served, we wound up chuckling like crazy. As each of us described an aspect of the meal we remembered we just about fell down we laughed so hard. I bet the girls still remember that night.

For the next few months, the relationship between Liz and Frank escalated. I didn't know they were fighting like cats and dogs until I came home one evening and Frank had punched a hole in one of the walls.

Whether that was the reason or not, Lizzie broke it off with him. For several months, he'd drop by the house, distraught. If Liz was out, I'd let the poor boy in and we'd talk about what he could do to get her back. I tried to explain that violence was not something Liz or I would tolerate. Unfortunately, anger management classes weren't available at that time. Eventually he stopped coming around or calling.

Then Liz met the first real love of her life, Jimmy. He was adorable, too. Blond hair, blue eyes, and he came from a nice family. No, Liz didn't have him fill out the form I'd provided, but we talked and from what she said it sounded like his father had a good job, his mother was a nurse and I was encouraged. When he invited her to the junior prom

Liz was overjoyed. "I have to have the perfect dress. I want to look really pretty," she said.

"You can't help looking pretty," I assured her. "You're young, you're gorgeous, and you have beautiful long hair. There is nothing to worry about. We will get you the most fantastic outfit."

We went shopping. When Liz walked out of the dressing room in a lovely dress, wearing stockings and high heels, I started to cry. The saleswoman was kind, bringing me a tissue, gently saying, "This happens a lot. We never realize they're grown until we see them dressed up."

My little girl had become a beautiful woman.

Chapter 19
The Streisand Fantasy Comes True

Maybe it's because I can't even sing Happy Birthday in tune. Maybe it's because I harbored a secret desire to be an actress (or a Rockette, which is pretty difficult to do when you're five feet tall). Whatever the reason, my idol was Barbra Streisand.

New York City is a wonderful place to grow up if you love live theatre. When I was young, my mom took me to see the Rockettes. What a thrill! Those women were unbelievably gorgeous in their fabulous costumes and awesome headdresses. When all fifty of them kicked their legs at the exact same time I practically swooned with delight. I dreamed of becoming tall and beautiful. I only managed one out of the two, which ain't bad, but legs like those would have been so much fun.

One evening my parents went to see Yul Brynner in "The King and I". They loved it so much they took me and my brother to see it. I fell in love, not for the first time, but the first of the two times I fell in love with an actor. My love of theatre was ingrained, never to leave me. Because of the asthma, dancing was out of the question and I quickly realized I would never become a Rockette. Acting was still a possibility.

Barbra Streisand's first play was "I Can Get it for You Wholesale." I was 19 years old when I saw this rather homely, skinny woman walk out on stage. I said to my date, "She sure isn't pretty." And then she started to sing! That voice! Oh, my! When she sang, not a whisper, not a cough could be heard; she had our full attention. Gone was the skinny unattractive girl. In her place was an amazing performer. And my admiration for her was established, forever and a day.

Years and years later when I lived in Los Angeles, my friend, Zena, who was the Administrative Assistant for an executive at Atlantic Richfield Company called me late one afternoon. Barbra Streisand was receiving a National Organization of Women Award for Courage. Zena's boss's wife had two tickets but was unable to attend the event so he gave the tickets to Zena. Would I like to join her that evening?

"Oh, wow, would I! But I don't have time to go home and change clothes," I cried.

"What are you wearing?" Zena asked.

"What I usually wear, a suit, silk blouse, high heels and a hat." Perhaps because I was short, and my hair was difficult to style, I wore a hat to work pretty much every day. And not small hats. I guess nothing I did in life was small. Large brimmed hats, sometimes with veils, all smoke and magic that added to my glamorous persona. On the few occasions when I had my hair done, people would not recognize me because I wasn't wearing a hat.

"No reason to change your clothes," Zena responded in the British accent I loved to hear. "It's not black tie; people will be wearing everything from jeans to evening gowns. We're in Los Angeles now, not New York or London." We loved to make fun of the way people dressed in southern California. I called it The Fashion Victim Capitol of the World.

So off we went. I drove my black Cadillac, pulled into the valet service area and we walked down the red carpet. I don't remember if anyone took our picture but everyone was there: Governor Brown, Mayor Bradley, Jane Fonda, other movie stars and famous people we didn't recognize.

Zena was right, the clothes were a mixture of strapless evening gowns, tuxedos, blue jeans with high heeled boots; you name it, they were wearing it. It was before the era of *bling*. This party had the real *bling*. Diamonds were all over the place, sparkling from ears, wrists, necks, fingers and ankles. Ooh la la! We were in heaven. No one knew who we were or where we came from. The Beverly Wilshire Hotel lobby was packed. Glasses of champagne were passed around. I guess if you pay about $1,000 a plate for dinner you get free champagne.

A bell rang and the guests meandered into the huge ballroom for dinner. We were sitting at a table close to the dais. Miss Streisand was nowhere to be seen. I started to worry. Would she even show up? Rumors abounded that she was hard to work with but I'd never heard she was irresponsible. Just as we finished our salad, a hush descended over the room. Instead of coming in on the side, Barbra Streisand was coming in from the rear of the room, walking past all of the guests. Zena and I turned to watch her walk toward her place on the dais.

Guess what she was wearing? A tailored dress with a jacket, high heels and a gorgeous hat. She and I were the only two women in the room wearing hats. When she looked toward our table, she paused a moment, looking at me. Was she acknowledging a kindred spirit? Did I imagine that look? Maybe I did, but I was in heaven.

From where Zena and I sat at a table close to the stage, we could clearly see everyone seated on the dais. In back of the dais on the wall was a steady stream of clips from Streisand films. It was awe-inspiring.

I had to talk to her, I just had to. Several men were standing in front of the long table where she sat with Jane Fonda, Mayor Bradley and others. After three tries, I managed to get close to the stage, just as she was getting up to go to the ladies room.

"Miss Streisand," I said. She looked down at me. I smiled up at her.

"I just wanted to tell you how much I admire you."

"Thank you," she said.

"I've been a fan for years. I saw you in 'I Can Get It for You Wholesale'. You were wonderful."

Mayor Bradley smiled, saying "Wow, you were there from the beginning."

"Yes, I was," I said, extending my hand. Surprisingly, she shook my hand, saying, "Thank you," again.

People stared at me as I walked back to my table. Actually, I don't think I walked, I think I levitated. I was in heaven for months afterwards. My gratitude to Zena never diminished. We are still friends, and anytime we talk we mention that glorious evening.

Chapter 20
Child Labor

In California, children can work when they are fifteen. Being such a workaholic, and short on money, I encouraged my daughters to become self-supporting to the best of their ability, even though it meant driving them to their jobs and picking them up.

My boyfriend of the hour, Roger, was a florist. Madi, being the creative one in our family, loves to draw, paint, do pottery and even enjoys knitting and crocheting. Knitting was not something I ever got the hang of. When they were young, I knitted each of them a poncho. The problem was I never learned how to do the purl stitch. Knowing how to do just stitch is pretty darn boring. One of the ponchos was purple, the other one pink. By some miracle, I figured out to put tassels on the bottom, pink tassels on the purple poncho and, you guessed it, purple tassels on the pink poncho. They were two and three years old, so they didn't complain.

Anyway, Roger gave Madi a job at the flower shop on weekends and sometimes after school. They needed help, especially around holidays. She'd clean up the shop, sweep up the debris, and make sure the containers holding the flowers had fresh water. Little by little, she learned the flower business. Roger was a kind man and was patient with her. And he had a good sense of humor. One evening she told me something that made her laugh.

"What did he tell you?" I asked.

Giggling, she replied, "A lot of people come in to buy flowers and they ask if the flowers are fresh."

"Yeah, I can understand. So what did Roger tell you to say?"

Laughing, she said, "He told me to tell them that if the flowers were any fresher, we'd have to slap them." Madi found this hysterical and watching her joy made me laugh, too.

Before long, they showed her how to make bows, and then gave her extensive training on flower arranging, which she loved. Once they felt she was proficient, she began working with customers.

On a Thursday night she and another woman were working alone. Roger was out making a delivery. A man dressed in an old jacket entered the store. Madi never knew if he really had a gun, but he had his hand in his pocket and pointed it at the two women. They were scared senseless.

"Get in the walk-in fridge," he demanded.

Terrified, they obeyed his command. With the door closed they could hear him open the cash register. Madi told me later that it was freezing in there and her teeth began to chatter. As time went by she thought she was going to die there. But then the man asked them if they would be able to get out when he left. Half frozen, Madi screamed, "No, and it will be your fault if we die."

To her relief, he opened the door and told them not to move for ten minutes. The second she heard the back door close, Madi ran out of the freezer and called the police. While she was on the phone the other woman, who was much older, stayed in the fridge, yelling at Madi that they were supposed to stay there for ten minutes. Madi could not believe how stupid that woman was. I had to agree when she told me the story. She learned at an early age that not everyone sees things the same way. And not everyone has a brain that is in good working order.

The police and Roger arrived at the same time. When the police asked Madi to go to the station to look at mug shots, Roger closed the shop and went with her. She found a picture of the thief right away. Later on, Madi found out he was arrested but she was not allowed to testify because they said she was too young.

"So why did they ask me to identify him?" she asked me.

"Honey, if I had the answer to that question, I'd be on television," I replied.

Lizzie also had some excitement at one of her jobs. Her first job at the mall was in a candy shop where one of her responsibilities was to make the candy, kind of like preparing popcorn. To this day we don't know how it happened, but she set the little stall on fire. Quick thinking prevented the entire mall from burning down, which would have been a real tragedy.

When she called to tell me she had found the fire extinguisher right away and there was no danger, the thought of what could have happened sent me into a panic. Visions of her trapped in that little stall while fire ripped through the shop, made its way to her long hair and burned her to death caused me to have a terrible asthma attack. I couldn't stop thinking about the possibility of disaster. She, on the other hand, was thrilled that they had not fired her. That job did not last long.

The next career she pursed was that of a waitress. This was a girl who complained if I asked her to help me in the kitchen. The job she got was in a local pizza place where the paper placemats also served as the menu. Maybe what happened was because I taught them to read at any early age, or because books were a big part of our lives, or because Liz was intolerant. Whatever the reason, when Lizzie ran into people who were either unable to read the menu or didn't want to read the menu or asked her questions about items written right in front of them, she went ballistic. Listening to her stories about how she related to the customers made my hair stand on end.

One night she came home, tired, cranky and with more than her usual bad attitude.

"What happened tonight?" I stupidly inquired.

"Oh, Mom, this family came in with four screaming kids. They made me recite the whole menu even though it was right in front of them. They were probably illiterate jerks. Then one of the kids spilled a glass of water all over the table and I had to clean it up, which took about five minutes. And you won't believe this but they were so dumb they couldn't remember what I had just told them so I had to read the whole menu to them again. I finally wrote down all the orders and then went to get their drinks. When I came back the guy tasted his drink and said he ordered a Pepsi and that was a Coke. He was a moron."

A long pause. Then I bit the bullet. "Did you throw the Coke at him?"

Lizzie laughed. She has a perfect set of teeth. She looked so beautiful that I wanted to hug her but I controlled myself. This was a serious matter, wasn't it?

"Tell me. I can't stand the suspense," I said.

Shaking her head, still laughing, she answered my question, "No, but I thought about doing that, believe me."

"Did they leave you a nice tip at least?" I foolishly asked.

"Are you kidding? They left me fifty cents."

"Maybe you're not equipped to be a waitress."

"Well, gee, Mom, I think that's pretty obvious."

Instead of being despondent over this, I was relieved that she had not gotten into a physical altercation with the group. Her attitude toward her customers and the human race became angrier and angrier. At an early age, she too was beginning to realize that a lot of folks on the planet have values that are different from ours. Sometimes when she related these incidents we'd have a good laugh, but most of the time I worried that someone would slug her.

The absolute worst job she had was when she worked at Macy's Department Store. They'd have these 12-hour sales and hordes of shoppers looking for bargains would show up. One night Liz got into a fight with another sales girl at the cash register. They each had a customer ready to check out. Both of the women were loaded down with *bargains*. When Lizzie told me that she and the other sales clerk almost came to blows I was horrified. The incident sounded like a slapstick sit-com. If my daughter weren't involved, I'd probably be howling. But it was my Lizzie.

"You were screaming at each other in front of the customers?" I asked, picturing the scene. What would I do if I were shopping and the sales girls got into a knock-down drag-out fight? I knew I would just leave. Unless there was something I just had to have!

"Well, yeah, these people are a bunch of jerks anyway and the other girl tried to get ahead of me to check out her customer even though I was next. What else could I do?"

Before I could answer or try to make sense of this, Liz continued, still furious, "So even though she is a lot bigger than me, I was not going to let her get away with it this time. She's always doing terrible things to me, running over to a customer when it's my turn to wait on them and sneaking in before I do to ring up a sale. So I got really mad this time. I was tired from standing on my feet all day and she'd been in my face at least three times. Why should I take this crap from her?"

"Liz," I reasoned, "are you crazy? Didn't they train you that you need to act courteous and calm when waiting on customers? How could you two girls fight in front of the people trying to buy clothes?" I couldn't imagine screaming at one of our clients at the law firm, no matter how tempted I might be. Liz obviously had a chip on her shoulder that came out at the work place. It came out at home, too, but I was used to it.

Our conversation continued. "Look, Mom, you don't know what it's like to work in a place with some low class people who act like animals. And the people coming to buy stuff are worse. You wouldn't believe how they dress." This remark coming from a girl who dated a guy wearing a dog chain for jewelry!

Chapter 21
Madi and the Motorcycle

The girls knew I loved riding on motorcycles. If I'd been taller, braver and had the extra cash, I might have pursued buying myself one. One of my friends, Ellie, had a motorcycle. Whenever she came by the house, the girls and I would get excited. Lots of people had bikes but I didn't think Madi, the quieter and less verbal of my daughters, harbored a desire for one.

One evening at dinner, she said, "Mom, I want a motorcycle."

"You do?"

"Yes, my friend Vinnie told me he could get me one really cheap."

Shocked, I stalled for time. "Cheap? What do you call cheap? You know we don't have a lot of extra money." Money was always an issue. We received $800 a month from Social Security because Jack died before the girls were eighteen years of age. Maybe I was too honest about the money. They knew how much money I made and they knew about the Social Security. Sometimes they'd ask me about it, trying to find out if I was being fair. Lizzie once did a budget for me which was extremely unrealistic.

They constantly bugged me about money. Eventually they wore me down and I made a deal with them. I told them I'd give them each $300 a month. I kept $100 from each of their checks for room and board. Each month I watched their spending habits. Liz would go through the three hundred bucks in less than two weeks and then I'd hear her asking Madi to give her a loan. Madi saved her money.

"Well, you got Lizzie a car when she was sixteen. I'm almost seventeen and I want a bike."

Shaking my head, I answered her, "No way, sweetie, no way. That is too dangerous. I'm sorry." I thought the matter was resolved. Wrong again. There was constant arguing for weeks. And then one day she hit me with the bombshell.

"Mom, I'm buying a bike. I've saved my money, and the guy selling the bike is willing to take half now and I can pay off the rest."

This was serious. After all the problems with Lizzie, who was now on her third car, I'd hoped Madi would be the sensible, reliable one. Remembering Lizzie's accident when she totaled the Mustang, I could picture Madi lying on the street, the bike covering her body. I lost control. I started to scream at her.

"Madi, listen to me. You are not getting a motorcycle. The only way you'll get one is over my dead body."

What happened next still surprises me. No, she didn't try to kill me. Instead, she told me she was moving out of my house and she was going to live with Vince and his family. I'd never even met these people. All I knew was that they lived in a crummy apartment a few blocks down the street in a less residential area. I didn't know how to handle this.

"Give me Vince's mother's phone number. I want to meet her."

After I met with the family, I realized what was going on. Madi felt sorry for the family. They were poor. Although we weren't rich, I had a good job and was able to provide for the girls. This woman lived on some kind of government subsistence; she had two children, all of them living in a small two bedroom apartment. Madi explained she would sleep on the couch. For two weeks I tried to talk her out of leaving. But she was adamant. Madi had become a rescuer. That role would sit on her shoulders for the rest of her life.

Once I met the woman I wasn't as freaked out. She was pleasant and seemed responsible. Plus I was tired of arguing with Madi, so I told her, "Okay, if that's what you want to do, I can't stop you." I knew she'd be back in a week or less. There was no way she would give up her room.

But she didn't come back. Life was easier for her living with strangers than it was living with me. And then a horrible thing happened. Her friend, Vince, a friendly, affable kind of guy, went to the store to get some milk. He always wore his helmet. Except for that five minute drive. He had an accident and was killed. When Madi called me, crying hysterically, I couldn't believe she had to experience the horrible death of her friend at her age. But I was relieved that she had not yet bought a motorcycle for herself. Fortunately, she never did buy a one. And she didn't come back to live with me for many years, either. After Vince died, she became a help to his family and lived with them until she graduated high school. Then she moved to Oregon to live with Jack's twin sister.

Chapter 22
Up to the Present

Thirty years have gone by. I have a lot of wonderful memories and some very sad ones. Madi stayed with Jack's sister for two or three years and started college in Oregon. That's where she learned to drive and bought her first truck. She still drives a truck. She finished college at Los Angeles City College, earning a degree in Social Science. For several years, Madi worked with children, but eventually she became weary of being around abused children and changed careers, becoming a legal secretary.

When I moved to Albuquerque she followed me. I bought her a restaurant, which didn't work out. When I moved to Tucson for health reasons, Madi stayed in Albuquerque, working in the financial sector. Her life seems settled in Albuquerque, where she bought a house and where she has friends.

After Liz graduated high school, she floundered, not quite sure what she wanted to do with her life, attending college part time in Northridge. She moved several times, never finding a place for herself in California. Whenever things didn't work out for her, she would move back with me. After they graduated I moved into a two bedroom apartment.

When each one turned 18 years old I gave them their inheritance. Although everything Jack had went to Marilyn, there was a small insurance policy left to the girls. They each got about $18,000 when they turned 18. Perhaps I should have withheld the funds until they were older. But they knew about the inheritance and as usual I caved in to their demands. The money didn't last long. Liz used a portion of her inheritance to buy a new car, a convertible. Madi held on to her money a while longer. If they wish they'd made different decisions at that time, they haven't said so.

Although I continued to hold well-paying jobs in the legal field, my drinking accelerated. On the morning of February 15, 1987, I looked in the mirror after a night of over-indulgence. I looked like hell. Staring at myself, I waved my finger at my reflection and said, "Honey, you have had your last drink." I never had another alcoholic beverage.

Once I quit relying on alcohol, life took on a different flavor. I stopped dating and went to AA meetings. The AA program taught me a lot about life. My sponsor and I worked the steps and little by little I figured things out. One of the 12 steps encourages the alcoholic to made amends. Among several other people in my life that had been treated shabbily by me, I've made amends to Liz and Madi many times.

Six months after I got sober, I asked Liz to move out of my apartment because we weren't getting along. Sobriety made me take a look at things I was able to ignore under a blanket of scotch. I thought she would move closer to her school in Northridge. Instead, when my mom suggested she move to Israel, she packed up and moved to a Kibbutz. One letter I received related how they had her climb a ladder and pick bananas wearing a yellow slicker. Talk about picturesque speech! Living on a kibbutz wasn't her style. Two months later I received a letter saying she'd moved to Jerusalem. That's where she met her future husband. When she told me they were getting married, I begged her to come home. I guess she had some of my traits because she didn't listen to my advice. Instead, she married, had three children and eventually divorced. She's had a difficult life.

Madi moved into my apartment after Liz moved to Israel. She and I stayed together until about a year after she graduated from Los Angeles City College. We had fun playing Scrabble and smoking cigarettes. Yes, although both of then hated to see me smoke when they were younger and begged me to stop, they both eventually took up smoking and smoked for years, another reason for me to feel guilty. Madi was easy to live with, agreeable and very neat. We got on well. Those years were quite pleasant.

In January 1989, I was returning from playing bridge and driving the brand new Honda my parents had recently bought me. Some drunk was parked on the freeway with his lights off and I had a terrible accident. The car in front of me swerved to avoid hitting the station wagon but I was unable to get away. Instead I slammed on the brakes missing the parked car by an inch. In two seconds I was rear ended twice. A young man got out of his car to see the damage to his car (a huge mistake) and I saw him get run over by two cars not ten feet away. Twelve cars crashed into each other. The freeway was closed. I was the only car in the pileup that didn't crash into the car in front of me, but I was rear ended at least twice. The horror of that accident changed my life. I never recovered from the emotional trauma.

Two months later, in March 1989, I met Tom Powers, a very sweet man. By then I had two years of sobriety under my belt. I had not dated once I got sober, believing men were a thing of the past. I was approaching fifty years old. But once again I was wrong. A year later, when Madi moved out to be on her own, he and I moved in together.

That same year I left Hughes Hubbard and Reed to take a position with Tuttle & Taylor, a prestigious Los Angeles law firm. Although I worked in their litigation department for a couple of years, when a vacancy became available working for Merlin Call, a probate and tax attorney, I took the position. With his help and my friend Pat Roughan's help, who was a probate paralegal at the time, I learned about probate and was of great assistance to him. He and I became great friends and still communicate.

Tom and I took a trip to New Mexico in 1991, the same year we stopped smoking. I fell in love with Albuquerque. I remember the exact moment it happened. We were sitting outside the Indian Cultural Center having a cup of coffee after watching native dancing. While we were enjoying the sun, great big puffy white clouds appeared in the sky. I hadn't seen more than five clouds in the thirty years I'd lived in smog filled Los Angeles.

Turning to Tom, I said, "Look at those magnificent clouds. Why don't we move here?"

Always polite, he didn't ask me if I'd gone crazy. Instead, he took my hand and said, "I don't think we can make that kind of a move."

A day or two later he took a trip to Taos. I stayed at our rented motel/apartment complex to do laundry and rest up from being on the road for almost two weeks. When he had not returned for several hours, I became bored so I called a realtor, telling her I was not going to buy anything, that I was just looking around. Of course, I bought a condo that afternoon. Neither Tom nor I realized Taos was many miles away and roads in northern New Mexico were not as reliable as the ones in Los Angeles. When Tom finally called about ten that night, the first thing I asked was, "Did you smoke?" If he had said yes, I would have started smoking again.

Instead, he said, "No, I've been lost for a couple of hours but if I'd found a store, believe me I would have bought a pack." We got lucky. Neither one of us ever smoked again.

Tom and I got married in 1992 and moved to South Pasadena. Merlin gave me away at the wedding. Because I had the condo, we returned to Albuquerque the next year. When we walked into the hotel room, Tom turned on the television. While we'd been flying the King riots were going on. Looking at the television, it appeared that Los Angeles was burning to the ground.

I looked at Tom. "Please, Tom, let's stay. I don't want to go back to Los Angeles." Moving to New

Mexico was not on Tom's agenda. On the plane ride home, I cried most of the way. That's when the idea to leave Los Angeles became rooted in my mind.

While living in South Pasadena, although working full time, I bought my first home computer and began writing novels. I was inspired by a writing class I took at Pasadena City College. My first novel was *Kiss My Tattoo*, followed by *Kiss Daddy Goodbye*. Tom was extremely supportive during this time, tirelessly reading and editing all the drafts. When the rejection letters arrived he let me cry on his broad shoulders. Later, when the novels were published, we had great fun with the book signings.

In 1997 things changed at the law firm. The partners began having heavy differences of opinions and I saw the handwriting on the wall. Even though I loved working for Merlin Call and enjoyed being a probate paralegal, my good friend Pat Roughan who was now with Coldwell Banker convinced me to leave the firm and sell real estate. Two years after I started selling real estate, the law firm folded.

Selling real estate from 1998 through the time I moved to Albuquerque was an amazing financial success. For years I'd been embarrassed because I had not finished college. I started telling people I received my PhD in finance when I started making six figures while selling real estate in the Pasadena area. It was great fun.

The intervening years with my daughters had ups and downs. Good things happened and bad things happened. Sometimes we fought and didn't talk for months. During this period, I made about eight trips to Israel. The last time I saw Lizzie was in 2003.

That same year Tom and I decided to part ways. We had an amicable divorce. I sometimes think a lot of my unhappiness came from the horror of the car accident and the fact that I was terrified of driving on the freeways. Maybe I had to divorce Tom in order to divorce Los Angeles. He and I remain good friends.

In November 2004, I moved to Albuquerque, New Mexico, where I'd dreamed of living since 1991. I lived in New Mexico for six years, but my health suffered as a result of the high altitude. In January 2011, I moved to Tucson, Arizona. My brother and his wife, Sally, were kind enough to rent me one of their properties, and to point me toward doctors who were able to help my asthma.

My dad died in December 2003, and my mom is now 91 and lives in the Ft. Lauderdale, Florida area.

Looking back at those years, I wish I could have been a better mother. I wish I'd stopped drinking many years before I finally quit. Perhaps all mothers feel this way and have regrets, believing they could have done a better job. I don't know. But the girls love me; they say they have forgiven me for all past sins. We now have loving relationships and I'm grateful to have them in my life.

Chapter 23
Don't Die Before Paris

During a recent telephone conversation with my daughter Liz, who still lives in Israel, I told her I'd send her some additional money. Her reaction was, "Oh, Mom, I feel bad when you send money. I should be able to support myself. I don't feel good taking money from you."

"Now, Lizzie," I said, "what difference does it make? I'm not depriving myself. I'm not living in my car yet, am I?"

"Well, no," she whined, "I just feel bad. You shouldn't have to send me money at my age."

"Oh, Lizzie, it doesn't matter. If I didn't have it, I wouldn't send it. And if I had been a better mother, you wouldn't be in this position. Plus, if I run out of money, I won't be able to send it. And, anyway, the money is yours eventually. If I die, you and your sister will inherit it."

With passion, she shouted, "Don't die before Paris!"

I laughed out loud! You have to understand that I have not seen Liz or my grandchildren for over ten years. Now that I am in my 70's, I cannot bear to make the trip to Israel. It's not too bad if you live in New York, but getting to Israel from Tucson can take two days!

So I have decided to throw caution to the wind, take the cash out of my IRA, and pay for Liz and my granddaughters to fly to Paris. Madi and I will meet in New York before flying to Paris to meet up with Liz and my granddaughters. I plan to rent a two or three bedroom apartment on the left bank. I've been to Paris a couple of times and love the city. There are many museums and other things I'd like to show them. You can imagine how thrilled they are with this idea.

All of us, especially my granddaughters, are looking forward to this trip. My daughters know that I have a bad track record of changing my mind every fifteen minutes, so they're afraid I'll change my mind again. But I won't! That's a promise.

Made in the USA
Charleston, SC
16 August 2013